RESTAURANT
REALITY

RESTAURANT REALITY

A Manager's Guide

Michael M. Lefever

VAN NOSTRAND REINHOLD
I(T)P™ A Division of International Thomson Publishing Inc.

New York • Albany • Bonn • Boston • Detroit • London • Madrid • Melbourne
Mexico City • Paris • San Francisco • Singapore • Tokyo • Toronto

Copyright © 1989 by Van Nostrand Reinhold

I⒯P™ A division of International Thomson Publishing, Inc.
The ITP logo is a trademark under license

Printed in the United States of America

For more information, contact:

Van Nostrand Reinhold
115 Fifth Avenue
New York, NY 10003

Chapman & Hall GmbH
Pappelallee 3
69469 Weinheim
Germany

Chapman & Hall
2-6 Boundary Row
London
SE1 8HN
United Kingdom

International Thomson Publishing Asia
221 Henderson Road #05-10
Henderson Building
Singapore 0315

Thomas Nelson Australia
102 Dodds Street
South Melbourne, 3205
Victoria, Australia

International Thomson Publishing Japan
Hirakawacho Kyowa Building, 3F
2-2-1 Hirakawacho
Chiyoda-ku, 102 Tokyo
Japan

Nelson Canada
1120 Birchmount Road
Scarborough, Ontario
Canada M1K 5G4

International Thomson Editores
Campos Eliseos 385, Piso 7
Col. Polanco
11560 Mexico D.F. Mexico

This book is a composite of the author's own experiences. Names, characters, places, and incidents are the product of the author's imagination or are used fictitiously and any resemblance to actual persons, living or dead, events, or locales is purely coincidental.

95 96 97 98 99 00 01 QEBKP 15 14 13 12 11 10 9

Library of Congress Cataloging-in-Publication Data

Lefever, Michael M., 1948.
    Restaurants reality : a manager's guide / Michael M. Lefever.
        p.   cm.
    Includes index.
    ISBN 0-442-25938-7
    1. Restaurants, lunch rooms, etc.—Management.   I. Title.
TX911.3.M27L44   1989
647'.95'068—dc19   88-12004
                                                              CIP

To Joe and Connie for the early years
To Laura for her loyalty
To Pam, Ranae, and Mary Ellen for their help
To David Umberger for his illustrations
To Juel for his wisdom
and
To Renee for everything

Contents

Foreword

Finally—an honest, informative, and fun-to-read book has been written that portrays what it's like to be in the restaurant business. The reader will relive and share Professor Lefever's restaurant-business experiences and really will be unable to put this book down until it's finished. Those who have been in the restaurant business will thoroughly enjoy reading about the same things that happened to them at some time during their restaurant career. I regret that *Restaurant Reality* was not available for me to read twenty-seven years ago when I opened my first restaurant. In fact, this book is a must for everyone who wants to open a restaurant and should be mandatory reading for every foodservice and restaurant-management student in America.

In addition to being completely honest about his restaurant experiences, Professor Lefever has managed to maintain a delightful sense of humor that is cleverly understated but prevalent throughout the book. His ability to laugh at himself and his mistakes in a tongue-in-cheek way is like a breath of fresh air for all of us who have made mistakes in the restaurant business and didn't know whether to laugh or cry.

Every meaningful phase of restaurant management is discussed in *Restaurant Reality*. The beautiful thing about reading this book is that it doesn't feel as if someone is trying to give a lecture. Everyone can simply read it, enjoy it, and form his or her own conclusions.

All of us who love and respect America's great foodservice industry owe Mike Lefever a big thank-you. He has truly hit a home run.

THAD EURE, JR.
President and owner
The Angus Barn Restaurant
Raleigh, North Carolina

Preface

Bookstores are full of manuals, how-to guides, texts, and success stories on how to manage a restaurant. All of these books talk about how things *should* be. This book is different—not only does it talk about how things should be, it talks about how things really are. My primary objective is to present an authentic overview of the restaurant industry in a fun and readable style. Another objective is to compare different management attitudes in a logical way that will help industry professionals consider different viewpoints when making important decisions. Finally, I want to emphasize the significance of both technical and interpersonal skills in restaurant management.

This book is designed primarily for industry professionals, from executives and owners to employees paid by the hour. But anyone who has ever worked in a restaurant will find the text both nostalgic and thought provoking. In fact, it will be a real eye-opener for anyone who has ever eaten in a restaurant. This book will be especially beneficial to educators and trainers by generating lively classroom discussions. Students from foreign countries also will find it helpful for understanding the inner workings of the American style of management.

The format of the book was developed with the industry professional in mind. Each chapter approaches the industry from multiple perspectives, including those of an hourly worker, a corporate manager, a manager trainer, a district manager, a regional vice-president, a franchisee, a franchisor, a restaurant owner, and others. The reader will learn how each level of management requires having a slightly different operational viewpoint while maintaining a common set of goals.

The material in this book may be shocking, with its emphasis on the good, the bad, and the ugly of the industry. But that's how things really are.

MICHAEL M. LEFEVER

RESTAURANT REALITY

1

How I Got into the Restaurant Business

Several months before I was born, my grandfather built a small restaurant for my parents from the remains of an old pony express station. Obviously I do not remember too much about that early venture, except through guarded comments from my parents and other family observers.

My parents decided within a matter of weeks that the restaurant business was not the way to treat a new marriage. You see, my parents did not have much restaurant experience. But my grandfather quickly dismissed their objections by saying, "It's just as easy as cooking for a big family at home." In a sense, he was right.

As my pregnant mother became increasingly large with me, she also became increasingly unable to work at the restaurant. That left the operation up to my father, grandmother, and various other visiting relatives. I am certain my father did not know why, or even how, he managed to get himself into the situation.

I might mention that everything seemed perfectly normal to my grandfather, who regularly appeared at the restaurant for a cup of coffee. I remember being told of his lecturing my father on how the apple pies should look—with towering domes filled with at least four varieties of culls, or apples so ripe and rotten they had fallen off the trees. My father's pies never quite met Grandfather's expectations.

Before my first birthday, my father got a job that required frequent travel and my mother took on motherhood full time, which eventually forced my

1

grandfather to sell our family restaurant. But it still operates today, between a new freeway and the old remains of my grandfather's apple orchard. The new owners stayed thirty years, enjoyed the business, and were tremendously successful.

You see, the restaurant business forces you to make quick but basic decisions about yourself. You either buckle down and get to work or you get out—and fast. The restaurant business does not tolerate indecision.

My wife, Renee, whom I met while she was a restaurant manager for a large resort hotel, also had a grandfather who was interested in restaurants. He made a bundle buying bankrupt restaurants, pumping them up, and selling them for a quick profit. "I'll always remember my grandfather standing over the grill with a cigarette dangling from his mouth, dropping ashes into someone's pancakes or hash browns," she says. As small girls, Renee and her two younger sisters were frequently taken to "the restaurant" to visit Grandpa and Grandma; in those days most owners lived behind their restaurant. "We always had steak or shrimp, but no one seemed to mind our expensive tastes," she recalls.

I will never forget when her grandmother told us about the time she heard a loud disturbance in the back of their restaurant. She left her post at the cash register and hurried to the kitchen. There she saw her son, Renee's dad, holding his father by the throat at arm's length. "He's going to whip me if I let him go, Mama," he said, his eyes bulging. Her grandmother explained that these frequent bouts almost always ended in a good laugh, and she preferred watching the cooks take their frustrations out on each other rather than on the customers.

Not long ago we visited Renee's grandmother again. She told us how she was always responsible for the cash. "I'd take the money home at night and put it in a shoebox until we had a couple of thousand dollars. Then we'd take the whole mess to the bank," she said. Things really have not changed much since those days.

From my own beginnings, I found myself pursuing a long career in restaurants. When I was fourteen, I started working as a dishwasher in a large, full-service Italian restaurant. I became the kitchen supervisor when I was sixteen. For thirteen years I worked weekends and summer vacations in the same restaurant. I have many fond memories, especially when Joe, the owner, would yell, "Hey, Mikey boy." I worked my way through high school and much of college in that restaurant. I did not know it at the time, but I was getting hooked on the industry while thinking I was simply financing a college education.

My next experience was with a fast-food chain. For the first six months I watched hamburger patties evaporate on the grill and jammed limp french fries into tiny envelopes. I became a manager and later trained other managers. Then I wrote training manuals, which described the process of tricking the customer's sense of smell and taste into enjoying a strange combination of elements.

Years later I ran into one of my former trainees, and we reminisced about the good old days. "Do you remember when we had two cash registers at the front counter with one cashier stealing and the other shortchanging customers?" she asked. But somehow we always seemed to balance.

I moved up to district-level management several years later, responsible for a number of restaurants in different states. The thing I remember most is the amount of time I spent waiting in airports and traveling between restaurants.

It was a tremendous learning experience because my background was in operations or the daily routine of managing restaurants. District-level management involves basic political skills and great sensitivity to other people's territories. I quickly discovered that good social skills could not always be substituted for good political skills. Corporate politics was a new and different ball game.

I experienced the next level of foodservice management in much the same way. As a regional vice-president, I did not seem to fit in as well as some of the more seasoned players. Again there was a whole new set of political rules, which might be summed up this way: The higher you go in management, the more important it is to be able to convince someone that you know something, rather than just plain know it.

I consider my experience in corporate foodservice management extremely valuable. It was like learning how to swim with my hands tied behind my back: those of us who were lucky never learned to swim; we just didn't drown.

In the years between my corporate positions of training manager and district manager, Renee and I bought a coffee shop at a busy corner in a tourist town. It was tremendously profitable and it greatly strengthened our addiction to the spirit of free enterprise. The coffee shop was the first of three successful restaurants we eventually bought and sold. After selling each one, we would say to each other, "Let's never do that again." But we always found ourselves looking for just one more golden opportunity.

Now I share my restaurant experiences with students at a major university. I watch their eyes light up when I say, "This is how it works in the real world." Throughout my career, employees have been my most valuable resources. They were all so very special in their own way. Today I feel the same compassion for my students.

As a young boy, I visited my grandfather in the summers and asked him endless questions about the restaurant he had built for my parents. Every day we would walk the worn and deep trail through the orchard to the restaurant, where we sat on high counter stools, ate apple pie, and talked with the owners. I would hurry through the crust so I could go outside and borrow a bucket and brush to scrub the brass Pony Express plaque mounted on a huge boulder outside the front entrance. Often a customer would ask what I was doing. I was always ready with my reply: "I'm going to own this restaurant someday, and I'm just taking good care of it now."

I never had to own the old family restaurant to feel its calling. At college, many of my fellow students would say, "I'm here so I never have to work in another restaurant." In later years I saw many of those same students. They were still complaining even though they had respectable, well-paying careers.

On the other hand, I find no greater joy than working in a kitchen or socializing with customers. Let's face it, you are too busy to be sulky in a restaurant. There is also something satisfying about managing a restaurant. It seduces you with a warm but demanding personality. In return for dedication and plain hard work, it will give you a feeling of purpose and totality. What I notice most is how time speeds up and seems to disappear.

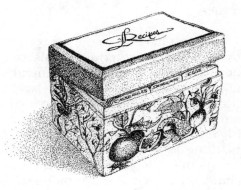

2

Why People Buy Restaurants

Grandma's Favorite Recipe

While on a recent vacation, I got up early one morning and walked the short distance to the seashore. As the sun formed a complete circle slightly above the horizon, I started wondering again how I ever got into this crazy business. Why did I keep buying restaurants when I promised myself and everyone else I would never do it again? Then an elderly woman approached and stopped next to me on the pier. "Good morning, young man. What a beautiful sunrise." "Yes, it is," I replied, nodding. "What do you do for a living?" asked the woman. "Oh, I own a restaurant," I said. "Just think of that," she said. "I owned one too, until I had a stroke."

I have always wondered why people buy restaurants. Why would anybody want to buy a job that gives you high blood pressure, varicose veins, and addictions to cigarettes, coffee, and alcohol? But maybe you have had a friend who sold his twenty-year-old home and used the equity to purchase a pizza parlor. Or maybe you are at a very frustrating point in your corporate career and just want to try something on your own. Your ancestors began at rock bottom and made it the hard way. There is nothing stopping you from doing it too, right? After all, you think, restaurant ownership is nothing but good, clean, hard work.

After that brief conversation on the shore, I began thinking again about why people buy restaurants and how they get themselves into a business that can be a silent killer. Most of the reasons I thought of were a mixture of hope and despair, anger and joy, determination and uncertainty. The restaurant business really is bittersweet, and so is the process of becoming a restaurant owner.

Do you have an old family recipe that you know is worth millions? I think most of us have entertained this exciting thought. The topic usually surfaces during holidays, when four generations are seated around mounds of yellow mashed potatoes, overcooked roast beef, sticky sweet potatoes, strange mixtures of green Jell-O and suspended vegetables, and an insufficient supply of red wine. One of the grown-up children says, "Don't you think Grandma's apple pie recipe is good enough to sell?" Of course everyone agrees, since Grandma is sitting down at the end of the table complaining how no one is eating enough!

As the wine disappears, the recipe for apple pie grows into an international chain with a thousand franchised units. But as the meal concludes with a generous portion of that apple pie, the topic always changes to something much less ambitious. Grandma does not seem to care or listen, because the same conversation happens each year and always ends when the reality of Grandma's apple pie is placed in front of the uncomfortable and sleepy dreamers. At that moment, everyone realizes how much work went into just one slice of that apple pie. Restaurant ownership makes nice dinner conversation—and that is probably where most ownership should remain.

For the past ten years, our family has been trying to duplicate a barbecue sauce recipe from a very popular rib house. We knew the success of the rib house was due to the popularity of its secret sauce, because the restaurant did not offer much in the way of cleanliness or service. If we could break the ingredient code, it would undoubtedly result in enormous wealth for us and all our future generations.

We started solving the puzzle by buying small quantities of the sauce, then taking it home to our kitchens for analysis. The taste-test panel, composed of all available family teenagers, bitterly complained about the forced participation and consequently refused to eat at the rib house again. We finally perfected the recipe by aging the disgusting brown sludge at room temperature in uncovered containers. The process involved several fermentations and frequent skimming. During this monthlong period, our house guests always found very unoriginal ways to comment on the offensive smell.

For the next several years, we frequently barbecued using our pirated sauce. Copies of the recipe were prepared and kept in several locations. The disturbing thing about this whole project was that our sauce never tasted as good as the original. Something was missing. Perhaps we should not have skimmed it. Someone commented that the authentic secret sauce probably was fermented with wild yeast floating around the rib house! Some people might call this the added value.

Even the sauce we took home seemed to lose its taste the farther we got from the restaurant. Grandma summed it up by saying, "My apple pie always seems to taste better at the county fair, where you can pick it up with your fingers and not have to worry about being polite." Well, our family never worried much about being polite anyway. In the end, we somehow managed to lose all copies of the sauce recipe.

The moral to this story is that while recipes are certainly important for your operation, they are usually not a sufficient reason to start a restaurant. In fact, many restaurants do not use standardized recipes or any recipes at all. When buying an existing restaurant, recipes often are not an essential part of the sale. The only time I ever worried about recipes is when we sold a restaurant and the buyers wanted to see them. Then we would quickly have to make them up!

So why do people buy restaurants? There are as many reasons as there are restaurants. Some might buy a restaurant because they like to eat. But restaurant owners develop very strange eating habits because someone is always interrupting them. Most restaurant owners snack constantly or wait until they get home to choke down some cold fast food in thirty convulsive seconds while watching a television commercial. Joe, my first boss, developed a habit of eating and drinking at his own restaurant. Each evening at precisely six o'clock he would sit down at an empty table and order a steak and exactly two martinis. But it was the only time I have ever seen a restaurant owner eat and drink on a regular basis. My advice is to buy a restaurant if you like to eat— but want to lose weight.

People also buy restaurants so they can have their own private bar. I have watched many of these individuals, and they usually follow a very predictable pattern. In the beginning, they do not drink until after closing. This lasts about two weeks. Then they occasionally have a drink or two with friends in the afternoon or evening. Eventually, their friends become anyone who sits at the bar. Finally, these restaurant owners may end up alienating their employees and family with their constant drinking. If it is going to happen at all, this final stage is reached very quickly, often within six months after the restaurant is purchased. There is really no compromise when it comes to drinking and owning a restaurant. You either do not drink or tend to drink too much.

Being a food expert is another popular reason for buying a restaurant. Food experts usually earn their titles by complaining the loudest and being unable to sit in most restaurant booths. Interestingly enough, they do not tend to hold up well when customers start complaining about *their* food!

You also might think you are a promising chef. Just because you can barbecue hot dogs for the kids on a warm Saturday afternoon, make spaghetti sauce twice a year, or spend ten hours preparing a gourmet meal for two, you are not a world-class chef. Many people are suspicious of chefs anyway because they tend to produce exotic, well-handled, and tepid concoctions in tiny portions.

Another common reason for buying a restaurant is the experience you gained while working in one as a kid. All I can say about this misconception is that kids remember only what they want to remember. The pressures of restaurant ownership are light-years beyond the magic of your first job.

An even better reason for buying a restaurant is that your wife is a good cook. What a wonderful opportunity to get her out of the house. Instead of watching all those soap operas, she could be contributing thousands of dollars to your disposable income. And she would still have plenty of time to take care of all those domestic duties such as preparing three meals a day without using any of the leftover restaurant food.

Then there is the potential restaurant owner with a friend who is a chef or manager. There is an old saying that you should never mix friendship with business. This is especially true in the restaurant business with its high level of tension, frequency of explosive situations, and convenient proximity of lethal machinery.

Have you ever known anyone who says, "I know what it really takes to be successful in the restaurant business?" First, it is no great secret what makes a successful restaurant: a good idea, a lot of hard work, and luck. Second, the uninitiated restaurateur probably thinks the key to success is a good accountant. But a good accountant is needed *after* the success, when you can afford to pay one!

"I know of a restaurant that went broke. What a fantastic opportunity." Does this statement sound familiar? This assumes that the prior owner was the world's worst restaurateur and implies that you are the world's best.

Once a restaurant has gone out of business, it becomes cursed. Local people stubbornly will tend to avoid reopenings. I have known these negative feelings to last for twenty years. My advice is to convert any failed restaurant into a gas station.

Other misguided restaurateurs want to specialize in a particular food or cuisine. This idea is basically sound, but it has one major and often fatal disadvantage. It automatically narrows your market potential and assumes you have done some pretty extensive market research. Also, it takes more time to establish a regular clientele for specialty restaurants. Finally, they require special equipment, which can make a resale especially impossible.

One of the more interesting reasons for buying a restaurant is to offer good food at lower prices. You might be able to do this if you have a fairy-tale debt service, but if it is such an obvious solution, why has your competition not already lowered its prices?

I should mention the front- (dining room) and back-of-the-house (kitchen) teams. These partnerships are usually happy little moments in the careers of budding restaurateurs. They receive cute and positive press coverage with the usual arm-over-shoulder photographs. These partnerships survive only in the best of conditions. More often, each partner begins to treat his area as a separate restaurant. Some interesting things can occur when this happens, such as internal competition, theft, arson, and hostile takeovers. Renee and I had a similar partnership. She was in charge of the dining rooms and I managed the kitchens. We had frequent squabbles, which usually reached their climax in the middle of a rush. During one of our especially heated bouts, Renee clobbered me on the head with a five-pound ham in front of our customers. They all applauded.

Many aspiring restaurateurs claim restaurants are the same as any other business. There are similarities, such as investment, risk, and know-how, but that is as far as I can stretch the comparison. The restaurant business can be better described as a very intense and unstable situation. The effects of mistakes are immediate and emotions are high. Moreover, you are constantly on display to customers and employees. One way of describing a restaurant is a business stuck in its adolescence.

Let's talk for just a moment about money and return on investment (ROI). I have often heard a prospective restaurateur say, "I'm thinking of investing in a restaurant. The potential ROI is tremendous!" There is no doubt the ROI is potentially tremendous. However, it is also extremely dangerous to invest heavily in a restaurant without extensive experience. Investing in restaurants is very much like investing in the stock market. Even if you lose everything you invest, you should always have enough money set aside to maintain your customary life-style.

How much money does it take to start a restaurant? The answer is about twice as much as the initial sales price or start-up costs. That is usually equal to twice as much as you have! All too often I have seen buyers use every penny of their working capital to purchase a fancy restaurant. When it comes to ordering food they use credit. They buy light bulbs with their charge cards, and load their cash register with change from a cash advance on their American Express card. Then the insurance agent calls and says, "We can't issue your insurance without the first quarter's premium in cash." There goes the children's education trust fund. No doubt the children will get a better education in the restaurant.

Exactly how much return on investment can a restaurateur expect? The only guarantee is lots of hard work for the money. Even if successful, most restaurants are not designed to produce impressive ROI figures. This only results in higher taxes. The only exception to this rule is the corporation, in which stockholders demand their dividends or return on equity (ROE). I will talk more about the hidden financial benefits in chapter 20.

How much risk is involved in the restaurant business? Estimates of failures range from 75 to 95 percent within the first two years. The amateur restaurateur must realize that many large business organizations thrive on mistakes. These organizations hire people to correct and control mistakes, while in fact these same people simply generate more mistakes. But the independent restaurant does not tolerate mistakes, and the impact is abrupt. So the restaurateur cannot afford to make any mistakes. For example, making an employee angry could result in tremendous loss by theft or fire. On the other hand, accepting a substitute brand of fryer oil could severely damage the quality of your famous french fries and give them—and you—a limp reputation.

There are many myths and realities associated with buying restaurants. One of these myths is the advantage of writing everything off on your taxes. In reality you can only *try* to write everything off. There are two basic approaches to restaurant tax write-offs. The conservative approach empties your already meager savings account at tax time, but it allows you to open mail from the IRS without fainting. The suspenseful approach, relying on very liberal write-offs, is much more fun. You can go on vacation with the extra money. This approach becomes even more suspenseful when you hear that the little doughnut-shop owner next door just paid twenty-five thousand dollars in back taxes, and you happen to have the same accountant and go on vacations together. Renee and I always considered ourselves lucky. We get audited by the IRS only every other year.

Another myth is that the restaurateur is his own boss. In a way, this is true. If a restaurateur is having a particularly trying day, he can usually just walk out, play nine holes of golf, and cheat on his score. This is more difficult when you work for someone else because it is your boss who gets to cheat at golf. In reality, though, every restaurant customer, employee, purveyor, government official, and stranger is your boss. Each time you disappoint or alienate any of these individuals, you are taking money right out of your pocket.

I remember when I first discovered this reality. We had owned our first restaurant for about two months when a regular customer informed me of my second-class status and his first-class status. You know, I never had the same affection for my customers after that day, and I certainly never forgave that particular one.

I already knew that employees enjoyed a higher status than owners. The government makes restaurant owners wallpaper the employee's break area with how-to brochures on employer entrapment (e.g., how employees can show up fifteen minutes before their shifts, wait in the dining room, and get paid for it). One of my employees penciled in equivalent dollar amounts awarded for each possible infraction by an employer (yelling at an employee might cost an employer ten thousand dollars in a civil suit, whereas simple swearing might yield five hundred dollars from the Labor Commission).

Then there is the myth that restaurant owners have favorable working hours and can schedule themselves off at any time. In reality, about the only time a restaurant owner takes a day off is for an appointment with the accountant regarding back taxes, the lawyer regarding employee grievances, or the insurance agent regarding increased premiums.

When Renee and I had our first restaurant, we got up at 3:30 A.M. and did not get home until 6:00 P.M., every day except Sundays. On Sundays we just slept straight through.

When we owned our second restaurant, I would arrive at 6:00 A.M. and was able to go home around 10:00 P.M. every day—with no days off. During those years, I remember taking off Christmas and several days when I was infectious. Simply being sick was no excuse.

Another one of our restaurants was much the same. We arrived at 8:00 A.M. and worked nonstop until 9:00 P.M., with Mondays off. However, I did not have the luxury of sleeping on Mondays that time. Our restaurant was full of antique equipment so I spent my days off whining to repairmen how poor we were and asking if I could hold their flashlights for a discount.

A common myth about restaurant owners is that they can eat anything, anytime. In reality they usually eat leftovers and scraps, afraid to eat anything they could eventually sell to their customers. Let me set the record straight. Only your employees eat everything all the time. Restaurant employees eat something off almost every dish that leaves the kitchen and even eat things off the dirty dishes. Sometimes employees carry food around all day in their hands, pockets, or mouths. Other times they hide half-eaten morsels throughout the restaurant like a secret internal buffet.

Another myth is that restaurant owners make many new friends. The restaurateur is really no different than other business owners. He will have many business acquaintances but seldom do those acquaintances develop into personal friendships. If the restaurant happens to have a lounge, many of those acquaintances will certainly act like lifelong friends just to get another complimentary drink.

We found it very difficult to develop friendships in the restaurant business because of the long working hours. Friendships did develop, but they followed a peculiar pattern. It generally took at least one year to start friendships and another year to develop them. The sad thing about this pattern for us was that we usually sold our restaurants after two years and moved to another location, constantly leaving our friends behind.

I should warn new restaurateurs about a small group, or cult, of customers who wait for new restaurants or owners. They tend to be overly friendly, stay too long, sit at the same table, and always order the same thing. These customers don't become friends and will disappear after a few months when they realize they are not the center of attention.

A final popular myth is that restaurant owners make tons of money. This is true, but they get to keep it only long enough to count it. That impressive wad of money bulging from the restaurant owner's front pocket is generally just cash-register change. We never seem to establish healthy savings accounts, just very active checking accounts. On the other hand, we never seem to run out of cash either.

I will never forget one of the small luxuries we enjoyed while owning one of our restaurants. It was being able to go to the market every evening for our dinner groceries. I truly enjoyed this European method of shopping. I would pick up a fresh baguette, a bottle of vintage wine, a few slices of imported cheeses, and some imported fruit. We never used anything from the restaurant because it reminded us too much of work. It was a daily ritual and we never worried about the expense. Now, on a monthly salary, we have resumed buying weekly commodities and preparing institutional food for two.

So far I have discussed some of the more popular reasons for wanting to buy a restaurant and some of the myths hiding the realities. Now I would like to share some actual case studies and tell you what motivated me to buy my restaurants.

I began working in Joe's restaurant when I was fourteen. I remember his constant complaining about how he got into the business. It seems he and a partner had come to town to open the restaurant. He had the money and his partner had the experience. Before long they had a growing and successful business. One day the partner began gambling and lost his share of the restaurant, along with everything else. Joe was forced to pay off the gambling debt and buy out his partner. The old partner kept coming around trying to collect more money, until finally he was escorted out of town by the sheriff. This left Joe with a restaurant but no one to run it. So his wife borrowed all her mother's recipes and they went to work together.

They were successful despite the way things happened. I do not think there was even one day when I worked there that Joe did not remind everyone, including his customers, that operating the restaurant was not his idea. I remember his chewing a cigar, drinking a martini, and rolling a thousand meatballs in the open kitchen while complaining. Sometimes he would not shave or change his sauce-stained white shirt so he would look more pathetic. He even blamed his mother-in-law for providing the recipes.

I know of another friend who managed a full-service restaurant for a physician. The physician supposedly bought it because his condominiums were not adequately sheltering his income. The real reason he bought the restaurant was probably to get his wife out of the house and out of the state, since they lived on the East Coast and the restaurant was on the West Coast. His wife worked in the restaurant for a few months until she caused so much confusion that she was asked by the crew to go home. She did, but the physician moved to the restaurant. I remember hearing my friend the manager say, "I feel more like a concierge than a manager!"

I once worked with a fellow for a large restaurant chain. We both stayed with the company for several years before leaving to buy our own restaurants. One day I called while he was working the grill of his hamburger stand. He said, "Remember those days we spent trying to locate the company's missing food and money. We were never really sure where it all went, but at least we made it look good on paper. Now, working for myself, I know exactly where the missing money goes—in my pocket, before my wife has a chance to count it."

Then there was the real estate developer who wanted to buy a restaurant so he and his family could spend more time together. He built his restaurant and enjoyed that part thoroughly. He then acquired a franchise, and his family went off to corporate headquarters for their two weeks of immersion training. When they came back they had a very successful grand opening. But after a few weeks, his kids became depressed and uncooperative because they had to work almost every day. One of his teenagers even ran away from home. She eventually came home on condition that she did not have to work in the restaurant anymore.

The owner realized he did not like working over a hot stove or listening to customers complain about the dirty rest rooms. So he returned to his former profession, developing shopping centers, and left his wife behind to operate the restaurant alone. She later was unable to sell the restaurant, so she just gave it back to the franchisor.

I also had the pleasure of knowing a gentleman who cooked for a large hotel on the West Coast. He eventually saved enough money to open a small Chinese restaurant with a counter and five stools. After many years of working twelve-hour days with no days off, he finally was able to buy a larger restaurant. We would stand for hours talking in his kitchen as he prepared hundreds of colorful and greasy dishes in his woks. When asked why he had become a restaurant owner, he said, "Each year I bring another member of my family over from China and give them a job here in the restaurant." He was also a very proud person who would sit for hours on a bench across from his restaurant and admire his building. The thing he always worried about while sitting there was the size of his family still in China, all waiting for their tickets.

Renee and I would usually operate our restaurants for two years before putting them up for sale. Sometimes we sold a restaurant within two weeks and sometimes it took much longer. One day a man and his wife came into our first restaurant and said they owned a seasonal restaurant at a nearby resort. They were interested in selling their restaurant and buying ours. They said they would be back in exactly a year to make an offer. Who would believe that someone would come back in exactly one year? A year passed without any solid offers on our restaurant—and then in walked the couple. They bought it the following week. I had to ask them why they had waited a year. They laughed and said, "We know how much work is involved in the restaurant business and just wanted a long vacation before we did it again!"

Some restaurant owners are in the business to feed their families, literally. The tax advantages are obvious when deducting food, transportation, entertainment, medical, and other expenses for a large family. The major problem facing these restaurateurs is that customers become a nuisance and take second priority. Renee and I have eaten in several restaurants where we were among the few paying customers in a dining room full of the owner's family. All the good items on the menu were already gone because "the grandchildren order first." Then we would overhear three of the married daughters, all nursing their babies, arguing over who would have to serve us!

We have known parents who have financed a restaurant for their son or daughter. Their motives are not always noteworthy. Some parents sponsor their children primarily because of the high risk involved in the business! I think they actually want them to experience failure. Other parents simply want the opportunity to rescue their children from the cruel world of business. Still other parents want the opportunity to come in and take over when they detect their children's predictable lack of confidence. Finally, some parents think of it as a final payment of their formal parental responsibilities.

I used to eat at a tiny lunch counter. People would come for miles just to eat the "natural" french fries. Every time a basket of fries would come out of the fryer, the owner would scoop in another large chunk of shiny white lard. One day he said he was going to open a second restaurant a few miles down the road. No one thought much about it until we started noticing that the owner and his wife, who also worked in the restaurant, weren't speaking to each other. When they did speak, it was not pleasant. We finally concluded they were buying another restaurant just so they would not have to work together. We were partially correct. Not only did they not want to work together, they also did not want to live together. Having two restaurants made their divorce much simpler in a community property state.

Renee and I bought each of our restaurants for different reasons. Some of them were very similar to those already discussed, although reasons always seem to be unique when they involve your own time and money.

Our first restaurant was a well-established coffee shop at a busy intersection in a resort town. I had just left a large foodservice corporation where I trained managers. I was convinced that I was not getting my fair share of promotions. One day I asked my boss if my name had ever been mentioned for a new district manager's position. He said, "Sure, your name is submitted quite frequently, but I never recommend you because you're progressing faster than I am."

We bought our first restaurant to escape the corporate roller coaster and to experience what my father-in-law calls "working for a living." Someday I would return to corporate life and become a district manager and regional vice president. The restaurant did indeed relieve me of the burden of corporate politics but replaced it with an unimaginable amount of hard work and unbelievable responsibility. But the trade-off was well worth it. I have never had any doubts about my own abilities or limitations since owning our first restaurant. I quickly came to terms with what I could do, could not do, and was able to learn in life.

Our second restaurant was a partnership. We had plans to develop a chain of family restaurants. It was a tremendous experience working with contractors, developers, planning commissions, inspectors, and financiers. I think the reason we decided to join this particular venture was that we had felt trapped in our coffee shop. It was probably a combination of greed, ego, and boredom. Besides, it was going to be a big operation, and I could hire someone to take my place in the kitchen!

Our third restaurant was something of a sloppy purchase. We simply thought we knew it all and wanted to regain quickly the freedom lacking in our partnership. As someone once said, "Partners who pay also want the say." We pointed to a spot on the map where we would like to live and bought the first and only restaurant in our price range. It turned out to be a difficult restaurant, both financially and operationally. It was rewarding, however, because of the lessons we learned and the people we met. We managed to survive and grew from the experience.

By now you have probably decided never to buy a restaurant. For some of you, this is very good reasoning. For others, you will buy restaurants and experience the exhilaration of free enterprise at its peak. The rest of this book, it is hoped, will guide you in making the right decisions before and after you buy a restaurant.

Above all, know that people buy restaurants, and keep buying them, because their eventual success or failure is a direct and honest result of their own backbreaking efforts. Even failure is an honorable and successful endeavor in our free enterprise system.

3

Buying and Selling Restaurants

Only a Handshake Away

I remember vividly the day we bought our first restaurant. Renee and I were vacationing with her parents, Ozzie and Marg, near a resort town. For a week, Ozzie and I had explored the possibility of buying a franchise but could not find a good, affordable location. Then, by accident, we saw an ad in a local newspaper from a restaurant owner who wanted to sell his business. That morning we paid the restaurant a visit. Our vacation was about to end.

When Ozzie and I arrived, there were dozens of cars and pickups parked around the restaurant and down side streets, blocking several fire hydrants and driveways. Ozzie said, "It'll be just our luck they sold it five minutes ago!" I was hoping he was right.

We walked into a crowded, smoky dining room and spotted two empty swivel chairs at the counter. We edged our way through the crowd and sat down in front of an open kitchen. We watched the owner, a fellow about thirty, throw huge plates of hash browns, eggs, and pancakes onto a shelf where the servers picked them up and threw them at the customers. Suddenly, a waitress who looked more like a grandmother appeared in front of us and asked, "Whadaya wanna eat?" Ozzie ordered homemade cinnamon rolls for both of us. (He often offers to pay but then also insists on ordering for you.) Two minutes later the waitress slammed the cinnamon rolls down in front of us and said, "You're crazy if ya think you're gonna get those things down without a cup of coffee."

After Ozzie finished his cinnamon roll and half of mine, we asked to speak to the owner. The waitress said, "Sure, I'll ask him. But he'll probably bite my head off for disturbing him." We watched as she went over to the pass-through shelf. She said something to the owner, who immediately threw his hands in the air and shouted some obscenities. Several minutes later, he stomped out and quietly stood in front of us with his hands on his hips. I guess he thought if we wanted to see him, we would know how to start the conversation. Before I could introduce us, Ozzie said, "He's my son-in-law and wants to buy your restaurant." The owner smiled and said, "It's a lot of work. You still interested?"

I agreed with him and said it probably was too much work. Then I heard Ozzie say, "What time should he and my daughter come back so you can talk?" What Ozzie really wanted to say was, "I've got to get this kid working and out of school so he can support my daughter." The owner said, "We close at 2:00 P.M., so come back around 3:30."

As we were paying the waitress, her face screwed into a crooked smile. "You thinkin' about buying this place? It's crazy here, you know. See ya." As we left we noticed a yellow truck pumping the restaurant's septic tank. Ozzie laughed and said, "Good sign—means it's busy!"

That afternoon, Renee and I drove into town and met with the owners. They lived in a surprisingly large apartment attached to the rear of the restaurant. They both looked skinny, tired, and pasty. We talked for a few minutes about the restaurant and then took a quick tour of the facilities.

Back in their apartment, we asked if they would accept ten thousand dollars less if we paid cash. Ozzie had coached us all afternoon. They said their offer was firm. Next we asked if they would leave their appliances in the apartment. They reluctantly agreed and we shook hands.

The owners called a friend who was in real estate. He appeared a half-hour later and drew up a binder agreement. We signed the document, handed them a deposit, and agreed to close escrow the following week. That is all there was to it. It was quick and clean. We had just bought our first restaurant, and I promised myself I would always pay for my own cinnamon rolls in the future.

A week later, at 3:30 in the afternoon, we met the owners at the escrow office. Ten minutes after shaking hands with the escrow officer, we signed a stack of papers and handed over our cashier's check. Renee and I were the proud and terrified owners of a busy restaurant at a busy intersection in a busy resort town.

I remember driving back to the restaurant and wondering if we should park in the front or the back, or just keep going. The restaurant was closed for the day, so we unlocked the front door and went inside. This is the moment every restaurant owner wishes he could remember forever, so he will not make the same mistake twice. As Renee and I sat on the same two stools Ozzie and I had sat on a week earlier, we talked about a new beginning while we each asked how we had ever gotten ourselves into this mess. We were going to experience what America was all about—free enterprise. What we did not learn until later was that our first restaurant experience was very unusual, because there were no surprises and we remained on friendly terms with the former owners. We had also forgotten there are much easier ways to experience free enterprise, such as an afternoon tour of the Statue of Liberty.

We kept our first restaurant for several years before deciding to list it with a real estate broker. He wanted a six-month listing and a 12 percent commission. When I told him I thought the first part was too long and the second part was too high, he just smiled and said, "That's what it takes to do it right." After a struggle, I managed to reduce the commission to 10 percent.

We signed the listing agreement early in our third summer at the restaurant. The broker kept his promise and advertised the restaurant many times in the *Wall Street Journal* and several of the larger regional newspapers. I never understood why he advertised in the *Wall Street Journal*—until it resulted in an interesting offer. Two gentlemen in Los Angeles wanted to trade their condominium for the restaurant. The condominium was appraised at only half the value of the restaurant, and the offer did not include any cash. This meant we would have to sell the condominium immediately to pay the broker's fee. Needless to say, we did not accept that particular offer, but it gave us hope. The story behind the offer was that the older gentlemen wanted to buy the younger gentleman, his jealous lover, a business far away from Los Angeles.

Once your restaurant is listed, all offers must pass through the broker even if someone walks in off the street wanting to buy it. This is precisely what happened. We must have had at least three different individuals interested in buying our restaurant until they discovered it was listed. When you list a restaurant, the price is usually increased by the amount of the broker's commission. For example, if you want $200,000 for your restaurant, a broker with a 10 percent commission will list it for $220,000. Many potential buyers think this adjusted price is unreasonable and will avoid restaurants associated with a broker. I think they are also avoiding the payment of earnest money, since it is often nonrefundable.

We did, however, have several people interested in buying the restaurant who did not seem to mind working with our broker. The only difficulties were their lack of cash and collateral. In fact, they did not even own their cars. Sometimes they were just drifting through town. Anyway, they claimed their vast restaurant experience was more than adequate security. It always seemed they had more employers than years on their résumés, and their financial statements were often prepared by the Unemployment Compensation Department.

We listed our restaurant a second time with the same broker, for another six months. That time we did not even get an offer to trade for a condominium. I remember getting pretty discouraged, because we had one of the busiest and most profitable restaurants in town. When our second listing expired, we switched to another broker, who came highly recommended and also just happened to be our mayor.

This person really changed my opinion of real estate brokers. I had never felt they truly earned their commissions. After working with him, I knew at least some of them worked very hard and were very conscientious. He spent days in our restaurant getting to know me, the operation, and especially Renee. Besides advertising our restaurant and recommending it to hundreds of hungry people, he worked the toasters on weekends. He actually helped increase sales to the point where we were not sure if we really wanted to sell. Everything he did was first-class, including the real estate agreement, which we negotiated for three months at 8 percent commission.

We did not get any offers the first three months so we signed up for another term. I would call him every other day and ask if there had been any inquiries. During this second term, he showed the restaurant to several older couples who had the experience but not enough cash. We were impressed with his integrity for not selling the restaurant to a retired couple in exchange for their entire life savings.

One morning he called me at the restaurant to say, "I think I have a buyer for you." It was the most convincing and optimistic tone I had heard from a broker in more than two years. The day seemed unending as Renee and I anxiously awaited for the prospective buyers and our broker to appear at around 3:30. At exactly 3:30, his car pulled into our parking lot. He and a very tanned, middle-aged couple got out and came inside.

I sensed these people had "old" money. I was surprised when I found out they also owned two restaurants in Hawaii. They wanted to trade one of them for our restaurant so they could travel between the islands and the mainland on business. They were also prepared to pay the real estate commission. Now I knew why our broker had been so prompt. They even came armed with glossy financial statements.

It was a rather inviting proposition so we decided to fly to Hawaii in three months to investigate. That was the last we saw or heard from those people. We later guessed they really did not own any restaurants; we should have known all along, because even Hawaiian restaurateurs look skinny, tired, and pasty.

Another interesting offer came in at about the same time. An older couple who had owned several restaurants thought they might like to buy ours. But they insisted on working in the restaurant for two weeks before they made their decision. They were experienced and seemed to have many friends in town. Besides, what's a little free labor here and there?

We agreed and they arrived the next morning at 5:30 with a load of pots, pans, knives, and recipes. They were both excellent cooks and, in keeping with their profession, they argued and fought with each other all day. I remember the gentleman telling everyone, including our customers, that his wife was really a wonderful person except she had never been the same since menopause. In another corner, the woman would tell everyone her husband was recovering from a stroke and was not doing very well. We let them stay for the entire two weeks, mainly because our customers enjoyed the entertainment.

After they failed to come in one morning, we heard they were at another restaurant. I guess they were just keeping busy during retirement. Renee and I also noticed that even though we were thirty years younger, we already talked the same way about each other to other people.

After all this excitement, we still had not sold the restaurant. I am sure it would have reminded any potential buyer of a mental hospital. One Monday morning our accountant came in to deliver our weekly payroll statements. He was a retired IRS agent and taught us more about accounting and "not accounting" than the Harvard Business School. We asked him, "How can we make our books more attractive to potential buyers?" He said, "One way is to maximize your profits and minimize your expenses." Buyers like to see paper profits even though they would never admit to generating any themselves.

So for the next six months we filtered everything we could down into the bottom line. I am sure we were the most profitable restaurant in the nation for those six months, and probably set new standards for the industry. Strangely enough, those costly profit and loss statements never helped our broker sell the restaurant. They did, however, give us greater reason to sell— just to pay our increasing income tax to the government. Thanks to our accountant, we were able to justify those erratic profits at a resulting audit.

As I mentioned before, suspiciously soon after our last real estate agreement expired, a man and his wife offered to buy the restaurant in exactly one year. I doubt we ever convinced our broker that we had no prior contact with these people. Anyway, our friend the broker agreed to help us with the sale for a small fee. The sale involved several balloon payments and a lease-option arrangement. However, our broker was very knowledgeable and did most of the legal work himself, with some help from a lawyer friend. All of the negotiations were friendly and everything went according to schedule.

The sale of our first restaurant was a sweet deal. It was good for both the buyer and us. However, the sale was similar to our purchase: it was too good to be true and really was not much of a learning experience. In fact, our first experience of buying and selling a restaurant probably did more harm than good. We were not prepared for the real world of business.

Our second restaurant, acquired later, was a type of partnership. Renee and I were the general partners, and the limited partner was a slick financier. I will never forget playing golf with him. Seven of us watched as he teed off first. The funny thing was he just kept going and never waited for any of us. Once in a while we would see him hacking away through the trees in the distance. The rest of us finished eighteen holes and waited for him in the clubhouse. Soon we saw him walking in from a strange direction. He asked us how we did and then added up his own score. After all, he was the dignitary.

That same night he took us into town for dinner and then requested our presence at an all-night poker game. I was beginning to smell cinnamon rolls again. I will never forget the look he had on his face when someone else won a hand. He actually intimidated almost everyone into losing. I did not know how to play poker, however, so I was not especially adept at losing. Unfortunately, I kept winning, and then I cashed in early because I was tired. I did not know business etiquette called for staying long enough for him to win back his money.

During the night, several serious poker players won some reportedly large sums of money from my partner. Things changed the next morning. He was extremely agitated and had to leave early. I thought of the tantrums I used to throw when my parents did not give me money to stop the ice cream truck.

I hired a manager who was a very bright and loyal young man. He had worked in our first restaurant. I also hired an assistant manager from the town where we were building the restaurant. She was very likable and turned out to be very helpful. Her uncle was a city councilman who later approved some very important construction variances.

I was amazed that we could build a $350,000 restaurant with little or no cash. The contractor bought the building supplies on credit, and we subcontracted everything we could. I remember spending hours filling out credit applications, being careful to sign only my partner's name when it asked for personal guarantees. We got our utility hookups, landscaping, equipment, and even indoor plants on credit. The only time I saw any cash was when we applied for licenses and bought the workers beer. We even opened our bank account with a zero balance and used money from my partner's charge card for an opening change fund.

Another memorable occasion was when our equipment and interior package arrived. The equipment came in three huge tractor-trailers. I hired a crew of six just to unload it. It took three days. All the equipment was heavy, bulky, and downright dangerous to handle. After we tugged and pulled it into the restaurant, we had the painstaking task of peeling off the sticky adhesive that protects the stainless steel from scratches. We wanted to store the pots and pans but discovered the storage shelves had to be assembled first.

We found the larger cooking equipment didn't fit, and we ended up knocking down walls and punching holes in the ceiling and concrete floor. Then it had to be reventilated, which required another fire inspection. Before the foundation was poured, we had rented a small, air-conditioned shack on wheels, containing a table and comfortable chairs for the building inspectors. Coffee, doughnuts, beer, and complimentary meal coupons were always served before, during, and after inspections. We took care of our inspectors and they did the same for us.

The interior package was even more exciting. It included the counters, booths, chairs, stools, bar, cash register stations, waiter and waitress stations, room dividers, planters, drop curtains, and so forth. It arrived in a small rented trailer pulled by an old black Buick. When the elderly couple driving the Buick opened the trailer, I could not believe my eyes. It looked half-empty. How could an elderly couple completely furnish a two-hundred-seat, full-service restaurant with just an assortment of boards and seat sections?

They warmed up a few Polish sausages in one of our few working microwaves, after which the gentleman took a short nap in the back of the Buick. Then just the two of them hauled everything inside within an hour. In the next eight hours, they transformed a dining room shell into a beautifully decorated restaurant complete with hardwood finish, hanging plants, carpeted walls, luxurious tables, cozy booths, and tasteful wall decorations. It was unbelievable, especially since I was still trying to assemble the storage shelves after three days and never did use all the pieces.

The restaurant opened successfully, except for the presence of my partner's brother-in-law. Supposedly he was there just to observe our opening procedures and then move on to build another restaurant. To our surprise, he moved his wife, son, daughter-in-law, and grandson into a tiny apartment close to the restaurant. He constantly turned one employee against another and complained about everything.

While he was intimidating the crew and telling customers not to come back until he straightened things out, his family would occupy a booth for the entire day and demand constant service and free food. My manager and assistant manager decided to quit when he rented the apartment for another year. They also did not care for his ethnic and religious slurs. Since my gentle recommendations to our now-unwanted guests were obviously not working, I simply asked them to leave or I would have them arrested for trespassing.

They left the restaurant and went to the closest phone booth to call my partner. He arrived a day later, after spending the morning with his brother-in-law and entourage. He walked into our restaurant in the middle of lunch and sat quietly at the counter. I said, "Hello, how did you find out about our great food?" I knew I sounded like an idiot. He flatly stated, "I've decided to let my brother-in-law take over the restaurant. You can stay on as assistant manager if you like. I'll consider promoting you to partner again after he teaches you a few things about the restaurant business." I replied, "Let me guess. You're here to present a series of motivational seminars!" I will never forget his face. There was a wild light in his eyes, which was at least an improvement. I asked him, "Would you like to hear our side of the story?" He interrupted, "No, I'm not interested. It would only make things worse." He obviously had an imagination.

I recall looking back at him standing stiffly in the middle of the dining room and hoping someone would hang a coat on him. He was dressed in a polyester three-piece suit. As he turned his back, our manager said, "Look at that! He has a hole in the seat of his pants." This is how I like to remember our second restaurant and my partner. It took a lawyer almost another year to dissolve the partnership and have our investment returned. As you can see, we were getting closer to the real world of business.

Soon afterward, we called a business broker who seemed to be advertising quite a few restaurants for sale. We made an appointment to meet with him the following week. He started by saying, "I don't have anything good listed right now in the category you're looking for." We wanted a medium-sized, full-service, established restaurant, preferably located in a mountain community. The broker continued, "The only thing I'd recommend is a small but very profitable doughnut shop located next to an Air Force base." He drove us to the doughnut shop. It was small and certainly busy. I just could not get used to the idea of getting up every morning at 2:30 to make those stupid doughnuts, and Renee worried that she would be constantly eating them.

Next he drove us to a pizza parlor and bar located in a rough section of town. It was also busy, and we had difficulty getting through all the motorcycles chained together outside the door. The customers either had a single dangling earring or a colored piece of cloth hanging out of their back pocket as if they were playing tag football. I needed to use their facilities but decided to take my chances outside instead.

The broker took us back to his office and pulled out a file of restaurant listings. He had one more that he thought might interest us and gave us the address. It was exactly what we were looking for, except the owners had not supplied the broker with any financial information. That did not worry us because restaurant books usually do not reveal anything except the name of the accountant.

Renee and I drove up into the mountains the following day to inspect the restaurant. It was situated in the middle of a quaint old town and had a cute outdoor patio overlooking a river valley. It was not busy, but the owners said most of the business was on weekends when the tourists were in town. It was just what we wanted.

We talked with the owners, and they seemed friendly enough. So we went back to the broker and told him we wanted to make an offer. We thought we had learned quite a few tricks about buying restaurants, so we wanted to negotiate everything. We also wanted to see the restaurant's sales tax reports and operating statements. The owners gladly provided us with the sales tax reports confirming their sales, and they prepared a special profit and loss statement just for us. I guess it was their way of giving the restaurant added value.

We really were interested only in the reported sales anyway, because we were going to project and estimate our own expenses. If anything, we thought they had doctored the sales reports to reflect lower-than-actual sales. They finally agreed to our offer, contingent on renegotiation of a favorable lease with the landlord and the usual approval of our accountant. We finally reached an agreement with the landlord after several days of negotiation and some eleventh-hour changes over the telephone.

The next step was to apply for a liquor license. After we were fingerprinted, photographed, and interrogated, the agent typed our names into the Criminal Investigation Division computer. We were declared clean and given a large poster to display at the restaurant indicating a change of ownership. We could not close escrow until we received the license, which took about six weeks. These were some of the longest weeks we had ever experienced.

In the meantime, we had a few other obligations we had to fulfill before opening for business. We applied for a fictitious business name (a legal requirement to prevent duplication of business names and to document true ownership for the public record) with the county and had the legal notice published in a local newspaper. The restaurant also had a trademark, registered with the state, which had to be transferred. Then there was the sales tax bond, which allowed us to apply for a sales tax permit, and the usual commercial insurance package.

Next came the city license, which could not be issued until the fire inspector, health inspector, and city building inspector signed our application. The fire inspector made the sellers install a new automatic fire extinguisher. The health inspector just shook his head and hoped we would clean more often than once a year so he would not have to close the place down again. But the building inspector had a fit because the ancient plumbing was in violation of the code. He finally got over his hangover and granted us a variance. Do not forget, all those inspections cost money too!

Then we had to contact the police department and give them all sorts of information in case our restaurant was burglarized or we were burned beyond recognition in a kitchen fire. Next we applied for an employer identification number, worker's compensation insurance, state disability insurance, and employee unemployment insurance.

We still had to open a business account at the bank, arrange for night deposits, and order a charge-card imprinter. We ordered checks, business cards, stationery, and new menus from the printer. Applications were also completed for charge accounts with the local hardware store and supermarket. It was all pretty routine.

The transfer of utilities, with their cash-only deposits, was very time-consuming, aggravating, and expensive. We were subjected to hours of assaulting music while on hold to each utility. Even with our perfect credit history, they wanted hundreds of dollars in cash paid in person at some remote office.

New restaurant owners usually join a few local associations. You can always drop your membership later when you realize they are very cliquish and the only thing they do well is establish and fuel the town rumor mill.

We also applied for a special federal tax stamp and filled out scores of applications necessary for our purveyors to give us five days' credit. Of course, the only problem was that we needed credit to get credit.

After exactly six weeks of waiting, our broker called with good news. Our liquor license was in the mail and we should prepare to close escrow. Another week passed, but no license came. When we checked with the Alcoholic Beverage Commission, we were told it had been sent the week before, but to the wrong address. We thought it might be faster to reapply and wait another six weeks, rather than take our chances with the Postal Service. Surprisingly, our battered license appeared in a few more days, and we closed escrow the next morning.

We arrived at the restaurant early to take an inventory. Both of the owners were already counting and weighing everything, including lettuce leaves and pickle slices. I trusted them and said, "Whatever figure you come up with is OK with me." I thought at least the inventory would be accurate and fair, since they were being so meticulous.

We also signed the equipment list, which contained pages of items. We did not insist on counting every piece of flatware and every salt and pepper shaker. Instead, the list just grouped certain items together and did not specify exact quantities.

We were very trusting of the owners and even had dinner with them the night before inventory at the restaurant. They ordered several bottles of champagne for themselves, because we did not drink. We supposed they were just celebrating. A pimply waiter took our order but never said a word. He was a local high school student—and that explained everything. Boys just do not learn how to initiate conversation until their senior year these days.

We ordered New York steaks medium rare. The waiter brought them out two hours later. We wondered if the owners normally drank every night for two hours before eating. The steaks had been *boiled*. I imagined they had a famous English chef in the kitchen. They were out of dessert so we asked for the check, which the waiter presented to me. The bill was more than a hundred dollars, mostly for champagne, and included charges for the owners' meals and desserts. We asked the waiter for accurate and separate checks while thinking how easy it was going to be to build up the dinner trade.

Escrow closed quickly and we became the proud new owners of our third restaurant. Then a series of events transpired that became one of the most valuable educational experiences in our careers. We discovered that most of the frozen food was spoiled and refrozen. The canned goods had been passed on from owner to owner, and many did not even have labels. More interesting was the large inventory of food items not related to the menu. The wine cellar was full of unknown brands that wouldn't sell, and many of the bottles had been stored upright, causing their corks to dry and crack.

An employee who also worked for the former owners thickened the plot by asking, "Did you know someone came into the restaurant the night before you bought it and removed some of the equipment and inventory?" The former owner had also given all the employees who were staying a pay increase, effective our first day.

We were in shock, to say the least. In the meantime, we had a restaurant to run. I went to the wholesale cash-and-carry one morning to buy a few things for the lunch rush. At the checkout counter, with a hundred dollars' worth of groceries already in bags and twelve impatient people standing in line behind me, the checker refused to take our business check. The former owners had recently bounced several checks at that particular store, and they were still using their old checks with our business name. I handed over a personal check instead.

Then I went to the hardware store to buy some light bulbs. I asked if I could open an account that would be billed directly to the restaurant monthly. The clerk said, "Sure, as soon as the other owners pay their account." I dug into my pocket for some cash.

I got back to the restaurant to find Renee and the manager talking. The former owners had "mistakenly" taken the recipes and would not return them or our telephone calls. According to our customers, they were also telling people not to eat in our restaurant. Finally, they were trying to recruit our manager and employees to open another restaurant down the street. The former owners had signed a covenant not to compete, and they would be in direct violation of that agreement. Our patience finally came to an end and we called a lawyer. We were about to learn much more about the real world of restaurant ownership.

Several years later, when we listed our third restaurant, the broker turned out to be a restaurant owner herself. Consequently, she always wanted to dwell on the weaknesses of our restaurant, as if she were in direct competition. Needless to say, she did not generate much activity. After our agreement expired, we changed brokers. We got an energetic agent who thought she could sell our restaurant within two weeks. During that time we had three serious lookers. Then our agent began her thirty-day vacation and handed our file over to her associate. We thought the change in agents would discourage our potential buyers, but it did not. In fact, her associate was much more professional and caring.

I should mention that we always had our restaurant in "camera-ready" condition just in case someone came walking in and wanted to buy it. It was extra work, but I was convinced it would turn a looker into a buyer. I would polish the stainless steel every day and replace vacuum cleaner bags on a regular schedule. You would never find a cobweb or burned-out light bulb in our restaurant. In the storage area, all shelves were labeled and all the products faced a certain way. It looked just like a grocery store. You could almost eat off our floors, and our rest rooms were always spotless. We would check them after each visitor. I also had a maintenance and painting schedule. It sounds compulsive and it was. Sometimes I would even ignore customers to stay on schedule.

We received four offers the following week, from the three serious lookers and from our new agent herself. They were all impressed with the way we took care of the restaurant. I caught myself lying, "There's really nothing to it. Once you have a system, it's almost self-cleaning!" All four offers were exactly the same, so we told the agent we would accept them in order of receipt.

The first hurdle was finding out that the previous owners would not carry a note for the new buyers. This meant that all the money we still owed on the restaurant would have to be paid before we could sell. We reached an agreement with the buyers to split this amount. This was fair, except we had to borrow money just to sell our own restaurant.

The next hurdle was the landlord. He refused to assign the lease. We asked him why he would do this when he had always seemed like a friend. He dryly commented, "You know I want your restaurant myself. I'll just wait until you give it to me or until your lease expires." We could have assigned the lease ourselves, but buyers tend to get nervous when they do not get the blessing of the landlord. I saw Renee talking to the landlord one afternoon, and the next morning the landlord signed a new lease with the buyers. Renee had simply reminded him that according to our lease, we would probably own *his* restaurant if he proved responsible for losing this sale. I will talk more about leases in chapter 5.

The final hurdle was the Alcoholic Beverage Commission. Our buyers were actually a corporation, which required a special investigation and full disclosure of the corporate books. This was finally resolved after several weeks of correspondence, and we began the six-week waiting period for the transfer of the liquor license.

We liked the new owners and hoped they would avoid all of our bad experiences. We let them take possession early and stayed with them every day for almost three weeks. We helped them transfer the licenses and utilities. I even introduced them to the owner of the hardware store and manager of the supermarket. We did not charge them for the inventory and even left several family heirlooms. It was a classic turnkey operation. Renee and I felt good about helping the new owners get a good start.

Escrow closed on our third restaurant and we promised ourselves never to buy another one. We finally had time to take an occasional day off, and we could even go on a vacation without constantly worrying about our business, employees, and customers. It was a heavy burden lifted from our shoulders. The days and nights even seemed different, mostly because we could now go outside and look at them without a customer following us with an empty coffee cup. We were going to retire from this crazy business and just get ordinary jobs working with ordinary people.

On a warm summer day several months after selling the restaurant, Renee and I were outside our house enjoying the sun when the postman arrived carrying a registered letter. I signed and noticed it was from the new owners of our restaurant. We were being sued for a large amount over a small disagreement. I dialed our lawyer's number from memory as school resumed on the real world of owning a restaurant.

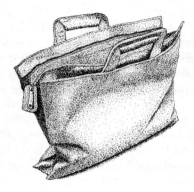

4

Franchising

What Disclosures Don't Tell You

It all started late one afternoon on the golf course. Renee and I decided to take a two-week vacation from my job as a fastfood manager trainer and visit her parents. Ozzie took me golfing the first day. It is a tradition with all of his sons-in-law.

He teed off from the first hole and made a beautiful shot down the fairway. Several people watching from the nearby clubhouse patio applauded. Then it was my turn. I did not have to worry about selecting a club because Ozzie lent me only his old four-iron for the entire course. I was just a beginner at golf and Ozzie said, "If you learn on a four-iron, you'll be all right someday." Instead of waiting for me to tee up, he started walking toward his ball and said, "Follow me." After finishing his putt, he began giving me a series of golf lessons that lasted for seventeen holes. I felt as if I had just split a cord of wood, however that feels.

As we walked back toward the clubhouse I asked him why he had made me start on the second hole. He chuckled and said, "I didn't want you to embarrass me in front of all those people. Besides, I didn't pay your green fees." As we tossed his clubs and my four-iron in the trunk of my car, Ozzie casually remarked, "Have you ever thought about buying a restaurant franchise?" I could feel my blood heating up.

That evening we made a phone call to the owner of a nearby, popular steak house franchise. We asked if there were any franchise territories available in the area. He said, "Why don't you visit one of my restaurants tomorrow morning and see if you like the operation." We wondered if *his* territory was for sale.

We got to the restaurant at 7 A.M. to meet the franchise owner. He had recently opened for breakfast and the place was packed. He wore several large gold rings on his right hand, was darkly tanned, had a big belly, and smoked short, slimy cigars. Obviously he did not spend much time working in the kitchen. Anyway, I have always been suspicious of people who smoke cigars in their own restaurant.

We had a surprisingly good breakfast, considering the restaurant was a steak house. Then we drove a few miles to his second restaurant. It was under construction. He explained how this newer building design differed from the older design. Specifically, it would have greater seating capacity, improved work flow, a more efficient kitchen, and less wasted space.

Ozzie and I were impressed with the restaurants and even the franchise owner, with his long, silver German car. We asked him how he had gotten started. "I just borrowed the money for my first restaurant, and it grew from there. The franchise company has been good to me," he said. That was all the convincing we needed. Ozzie and I thanked him and said we would be in touch soon.

We were consumed with excitement. Ozzie passed on curves and I gobbled two rolls of Tums on the way home. We decided to call the franchise company the next morning to inquire about the availability of a territory. That evening Ozzie played nine holes of golf and I played eight.

Early the next morning, we called company headquarters. We were quickly connected with the vice-president for franchise development. We told him of our interest in a particular area surrounding a small town. He said the franchise owner whom we met had first right of refusal on that particular area. If he released his option, then we could apply for the territory. The franchise owner must have liked us because he agreed to release his option the next day and recommended us to the vice-president. I was thankful it only took a few phone calls and not another car trip with Ozzie driving.

We were invited to company headquarters the following week. As an incentive, the company offered to refund the amount of our airline tickets if we purchased a franchise. The vice-president of franchise development greeted us at the airport. Ozzie and I were dressed in three-piece suits and carried leather attaché cases. Mine was empty. The vice-president was friendly and professional. He chauffeured us to an impressive, modern corporate head-quarters building.

He introduced us to the chairman of the board, president and chief executive officer, and, finally, the chief financial officer. All three were pleasant but busy. I wondered if they were really pleasant and really busy. We talked with the franchise vice-president for several hours. He was mainly interested in my experience, our financing, and our progress in locating a site. My experience seemed to satisfy them, although I got the feeling they thought I might have too much experience when it came time to share the profits.

Ozzie and I worked on our personal financial statements together so they added up to the necessary amount. We were thankful for the vice-president's singular interest in the bottom line of our statements and not the details. We also had three potential sites with pictures and descriptions. Unknown to him, the pictures and descriptions did not match, but we were selling ourselves, not real estate.

The vice-president seemed to be quite frank with us. He explained the franchise-owner selection process, saying half of those interviewed were usually rejected because of inadequate foodservice management experience. He explained how prospective franchise owners are often too stubborn to hire an experienced manager. He also was concerned with our advertising area of dominant influence (ADI). Our franchise territory might be located too far from a major metropolitan area and its television advertising capability. He also discussed the uncertain future market for red meat and how his company was adapting different menus to prevent sales erosion. Finally, he expressed some concern about the commodities market and the size of cattle herds. It was all interesting, and we appreciated his honesty.

For lunch he took us to a company-owned unit that served as one of their training stores for new franchise owners. As with most training stores, there seemed to be more employees than customers. If anything, we got too much attention. We talked to the manager, who was twenty-five going on forty-five. He said, "I really enjoy working for the company and having the opportunity to train new franchise owners. But being next door to corporate headquarters is frustrating and uncomfortable."

Every time one of several hundred company employees registered even a minor complaint or thought of something different, it would send the manager and his restaurant into a tailspin. As the manager put it, "It wouldn't be so bad except most of the company employees eat here every day because they get a discount." The manager disappeared and then the vice-president started complaining about the manager's complaining.

Right then we should have begun to worry, but we returned to corporate headquarters for a series of interviews and clarification meetings. We began with the accounting and data processing departments. It was responsible for invoices and payroll. All checks and payments from franchise owners were issued through corporate headquarters. This meant that the company had unrestricted access to franchise owners' bank accounts. There was also an optional feature that supplied the franchise owner with weekly profit and loss statements. These services required an additional fee above and beyond the initial franchise fee and the monthly royalties. They also gave the company ultimate control over the franchise owner.

Next we visited the design and equipment departments. Depending on the size and shape of your land parcel, there were several building models from which to choose. Seven copies of blueprints were included in the initial franchise fee. The company also had an equipment package specifically designed for each model. The equipment package was optional but recommended since it was custom-made to fit the building style—or maybe the buildings were designed to fit the equipment. Either way, we were locked into both. I had left my attache case in the vice-president's office and he kindly returned it to me at that point, probably wondering why it was so light.

Our next stop was the legal and real estate department. The staff attorney was available to help us negotiate any contracts or leases at no additional charge. He was also there for other purposes, which we would discover later. The real estate person helped the franchise owners appraise any land or existing buildings. He also made personal site evaluations. Sometimes the company would buy the land and building and lease it back to the franchise owner as an additional service (often called a lease-back arrangement).

Then we were ushered into the marketing department, where a representative explained the system. An additional percentage of gross revenues was required of all franchise owners to participate in the company advertising program, which included regional television and radio spots—assuming you were close enough to a major metropolitan area. If not, the company would substitute equivalent newspaper couponing and direct-mail advertising in our area. It was explained how marketing tends to be an inexact science and that the results often cannot be measured. The only measurable result was the franchise owner's monthly contribution.

Next was the operations department. It was not much of an office, just a few comfortable chairs and a table. We were not surprised, because operations personnel are supposed to spend their time away from the office. I can always spot a corporate operations person. They usually smoke, drink, or talk too much. The vice-president of operations was tense and fit the mold. His department provided a crew to help open the restaurant for the first week. He would personally visit our restaurant once a year, and an area representative would make monthly visits. He asked us more questions than the others because we would be his responsibility long after everyone else quickly finished with us.

He asked if I had thought about an assistant manager. Ozzie said that we had one in mind. Unfortunately, I knew that Ozzie was referring to me. The vice-president was very much relieved. He said, "I'm really glad to hear that. Some franchise owners think they can do everything themselves, and I end up being their assistant manager." We were glad to move on. Just being in the same room with an operations vice-president makes you tired.

Next we visited the commissary, where much of the food was purchased, produced, or packaged for shipment to the hundreds of franchised and company-owned units. All menu items had to be approved. This often made the company commissary the only available source of products. Ozzie quietly said to me, "I wonder if they'd consider franchising their commissary?"

The last stop was the cashier. The franchise vice-president informed us that each department representative had given approval and that we were being offered a franchise territory. We could close the deal in exchange for our five-figure cashier's check. What exactly would we get for our money? The package included two round-trip airline tickets, two site evaluations, and seven sets of blueprints. The right to use the company logo, opening assistance, and long-term assistance would be charged to our monthly royalties. Advertising and accounting would be charged to additional monthly fees. As card-carrying franchise owners, we would also be forced to purchase our equipment and supplies at prices often above market level and subject to company rent increases if we accepted a lease-back arrangement. Finally, we would be required to purchase expensive equipment (to prepare new menu items) throughout the life of the franchise.

Ozzie and I had brought a cashier's check but decided to hedge and ask for a thirty-day extension. The franchise vice-president was disappointed but granted our request. Surprisingly, the royalty rate, service fees, and initial franchise fee were not the critical factors in our decision to postpone the franchise purchase. What really worried us was something the company real estate representative had said about sewer systems. The cost of septic systems was often prohibitive for new restaurants, and our prospective sites were not connected to the city sewer system.

Ozzie and I thanked the franchise vice-president for his hospitality. We asked if he could give us any operating statements from other franchise owners. He said the statements were confidential, but he could provide us with a *pro forma* or standard company operating statement with fictitious amounts. The full-disclosure laws had severely limited the type and amount of information available to prospective franchise owners. The new laws were designed to prevent franchise companies from intentionally or unintentionally misleading prospective franchise owners with attractive operating statements. The vice-president did, however, offer us detailed information about the company and its officers. It was somewhat unsettling to see that all the directors were lawyers and financiers with little or no foodservice management experience.

Before catching our return flight, Ozzie wanted to show me around the city. He was stationed there as a pilot in World War II. We walked about fifteen miles to see if a restaurant was still there after forty-five years. Not surprisingly, even the neighborhood was gone. We caught a bus back to the airport. After stepping up and depositing my coins, I looked back at Ozzie forcing a folded dollar bill into the fare box. The driver was yelling that it did not take paper money. Ozzie's paper dollar jammed the machine, and the driver turned into a maniac on wheels. We got off as soon as we could and did not talk much on the walk back to the airport.

Ozzie and I never exercised our thirty-day option on the franchise territory. One of our possible sites had poor access, another lacked the land area necessary for a septic system, and another had a low traffic count. The company did, however, give us first right of refusal, just to keep us interested.

My second experience with franchising was mostly just an observation. Across from our first restaurant was an old, vacant motel. One day bulldozers appeared and created a giant dust storm for two weeks as they leveled the lot. The inside of our restaurant became coated with mud when the dust mixed with the steam from the kitchen. Then flatbed trucks came with preassembled walls. Within a few more weeks, we had a national fast-food restaurant franchise across the street. The most interesting part about the construction was that the outside landscaping was finished before the roof. We watched as trucks unloaded supplies on expensive shrubs, ran over sprinkler heads, and mashed newly placed sod.

The last official responsibility of the builder was to install the drive-through speaker box. We did not really think too much of it at the time, but that speaker box quickly became a public nuisance. All day we would hear the shrill and tinny, "May I take your order, please?" The speaker box especially bothered the neighbors late at night until one of them, the local newspaper publisher, called the mayor. The use of speaker boxes after 10 P.M. became a misdemeanor at the next city council meeting.

Renee and I were not invited to the grand opening. I suppose the franchise owner thought our restaurant, just across the street, was a little too close for healthy competition. He was busy for the first two weeks and then started to slow down. This is a common pattern for new restaurants.

After convincing myself they were not stealing our customers, I finally went over and ordered two sacks full of hamburgers, french fries, onion rings, and apple turnovers to go. I always order fast food by the sack because that is the only identifiable thing when you get home. Everything inside just seems to naturally melt together into a greasy sludge. The franchise owner recognized me and was surprisingly friendly.

As the months passed, our restaurant became busier while the franchise owner struggled with declining sales. It did not seem to make much sense, because the franchise company was large and enjoyed a good reputation. But our community seemed to support only the mom-and-pop businesses like ours. The more his business deteriorated, the more frequently he would come over to our restaurant and drink the generic beer we used in our pancake batter.

One day his sewer line clogged up, and we spent hours trying to find the grease trap. He finally had to close the restaurant. Business was so slow it really did not matter anyway. A crew finally dug up his parking lot because the builder had paved over the gas and water valves along with the grease-trap access. His line had clogged because a group of teenagers had stuffed paper towels down the toilet. He installed an electric hand dryer the next week. Just about the time he reopened the restaurant, a heavy ceiling chandelier fell on his wife, sending her to the hospital. She was lucky and required only a neck brace for six months.

The thing he hated most about his franchise was the bookkeeping. It was organized and simple but time-consuming and slow. His suppliers and employees were paid by check from company headquarters. Often there was a six-week delay, which kept the employees complaining and the phone ringing from angry suppliers.

He had a franchise representative who visited once or twice a month. The representative's job was to suggest ways for increasing sales and improving operation efficiency. His real job was to maintain continuity among the restaurants and to monitor the franchise owner's accounting procedures. In other words, the company did not want one of its franchise owners to damage the corporate image by producing an inferior product. It also wanted to prevent the franchise owners from skimming sales and reducing royalties.

The franchise representative's conflict of interest between helping and controlling often created a set of double standards. The franchise owner followed policy only during company inspections and even kept two different menu boards and a personal cash register hidden in the storeroom.

After a year, the franchise owner quit working in his restaurant. He would just sit in a window booth in our restaurant and look across the street. Occasionally we would go together and replace the rubber bell hose for the drive-through window when someone cut it off. After a while he did not even bother replacing it. Cars would stop at the speaker box and then drive away because no one would answer.

Then one day the franchise owner told me he had hired a manager. It was a strange agreement because the manager did not get a salary, only a percentage of sales *increases*. I knew it would not work, but at least the franchise owner was finally smiling. The new manager began appearing in our restaurant early in the morning and watched our cooks prepare the breakfast orders. Several days later, I saw the manager and franchise owner hang a banner on the outside of their restaurant announcing Opening for Breakfast Soon. They were convinced that our big breakfast portions were responsible for our success, and they were going to do the same thing across the street. Interestingly enough, the new manager never noticed the missing bell hose.

Early the next morning, the franchise owner walked in the back door of our restaurant and asked, "Could we use your kitchen for a few hours in the evening when you're not busy?" When I asked why, he said, "I don't have any breakfast equipment and want to prepare everything over here." I believe in helping my neighbor, but that was ridiculous. I tried being polite and replied, "I just think there'd be too much confusion." The next day we saw an equipment rental company unloading boxes, a dangerous-looking propane burner, and a thirty-gallon pot.

I was there to watch when they opened for breakfast a week later at 9:00 A.M. In our community everyone was finished with breakfast by 7:00 A.M., so their only customer was me. They had boiled fifty pounds of potatoes and grated them by hand. The manager had brought his two-slice toaster from home and they had scrambled four dozen eggs. They saved everything, including the eggs, until the next day and tried opening at 6:00 A.M. instead.

The only menu choice was The Works, which included a pound of greasy hash browns, four greenish scrambled eggs, two slices of cold toast buttered with yellow grease, fried bologna, and two stiff pancakes. Our restaurant had a good reputation for gigantic portions, so they made their portions even bigger. We watched from our restaurant as the first customer drove up to the speaker box and waited. They finally noticed the customer and got the order out thirty minutes later. At least the customer was smart enough to turn off his engine. The food was so heavy that it broke the Styrofoam carryout container and spilled into the car when the manager handed it out the drive-through window.

The fire marshal visited the franchise owner's restaurant the next day and advised him that having an unvented propane burner in the storeroom was a code violation. The manager reduced the breakfast menu to coffee and toast the next day. Their toaster broke soon afterward, and they changed again to coffee and Danish. They discontinued breakfast service the next week, and the manager never did get a paycheck. But he did become one of our regular customers.

The franchise owner called company headquarters soon thereafter and asked for help. He was quickly connected to the marketing department. After listening to his story, the marketing director decided to visit the restaurant personally. A week later the marketing director arrived, and he stayed two days in his motel room making phone calls. I had an opportunity to talk with him. He said, "I did a quick telephone survey and will send the results as soon as I can." It was quick, all right, whatever he did. After two weeks the franchise owner received a brief letter and a copy of the survey results. The survey indicated that people in the community liked fast-food hamburgers and that people who had eaten at the franchise owner's restaurant were generally pleased. The cover letter suggested a sales blitz and couponing.

The franchise owner had his kids stick advertisements under the windshield wipers of parked cars. That did not work because everyone started complaining about the litter when the car owners tossed the advertisements on the ground. The half-off coupons were popular and increased everything tremendously except profits. When the couponing stopped, so did the customers.

He eventually decided to sell his franchise. But the company was not interested in buying it and was not especially helpful. This started a lengthy battle between the franchise owner and the company. The franchise owner closed the bank account that was accessible by the company, turned-off the company cash registers, and did not return any phone calls. The company executives found a buyer within a week. The franchise owner walked out the door of his franchise for the last time, having lost his dignity and life savings.

The new owner worked hard and lost only his initial investment after six months. The company finally sold the restaurant to another hamburger chain.

I also had the opportunity to experience franchising from the company's perspective, as a franchise district manager. Let me start by explaining the difference between two types of district-level management. Most restaurant chains have franchised units and company-owned units. Franchise district managers (often called area representatives) have to be somewhat gentler with their suggestions since they are dealing within a form of partnership. On the other hand, company-owned district managers often act in the capacity of general manager and are either called district managers, area managers, or regional managers, depending on the number of units. I think the biggest differences between the two types is that franchise district managers work with older and more mature people.

Company-owned district managers are generally friendly people who come from many backgrounds and often work their way up the corporate ladder while remaining in the same company. I always enjoyed them as personal friends but not as business associates. They probably felt the same way about me. I always had trouble mixing corporate politics with restaurant operations because they are almost exact opposites. Corporate politics involve gentle massaging and indirect approaches to short-term objectives. Restaurant operations involve frequent and often abrupt approaches to long-term objectives. Career company-owned district managers survive because they necessarily concentrate on the politics and not the operations.

Franchise district managers spend most of their time traveling between their units. If I was not in a car, a plane, an airport or motel room, I was in a staff meeting. A good district manager has the ability to motivate a franchise owner while convincing him that he is being helped, not just spied on.

The franchise district manager also is responsible for reporting franchise violations to company headquarters. These include menu items, supplies, cooking techniques, accounting procedures, and anything else the company labels *unauthorized.* That always made sense to me, because a set of standards must be enforced or your company will quickly become a collection of mom-and-pop cafes and lose its national image.

If the franchise owner fails to correct violations or repeatedly violates conditions or terms of the franchise contract, the district manager has the unpleasant task of building a case. Luckily I had only one such situation. He was a particularly obnoxious franchise owner whom we nicknamed the Snake. As a new district manager, I was thrown into the middle of a long-standing feud between him and the company. I tried being nice. I tried being tough. I even tried being wishy-washy. I think he and the company enjoyed watching me get tossed around in the middle. I added a little spice by sending a letter notifying him that his franchise had been terminated and the company attorney would be ready with the necessary papers in two days. I do not think I had the authority to initiate the termination, but it was fun anyway.

The morning after he received my letter, he was waiting in his car outside my office. I was so worried he might shoot me that I stumbled into a squirrel hole and broke my foot. I looked up and saw the Snake sitting in his car and smiling as I hobbled inside. Our attorney failed to show up, and the franchise owner threatened to sue the chairman of the board if we continued the termination. I went to the hospital for X rays and returned to find the franchise owner reassigned to another district manager.

Staff meetings usually were held every month at company headquarters. Most district managers had to fly in for meetings, which often turned into big parties. Each district manager discussed his units and any particularly difficult problems. The franchise vice-president usually discussed issues dealing with franchise contracts, real estate, construction, leasing, financing, and especially any franchise owner who was behind in royalty payments. After the meeting, the party began. If the staff meeting was scheduled for two days, the second day usually consisted of training seminars and product demonstrations. Very rarely would the second day require any participation or concentration from the company representatives.

Franchise owner association meetings were much more exciting. The discussion almost always centered around the unethical practices of the company and its army of mindless and merciless franchise district managers. I have been to meetings where we just sat and took what we deserved. I have listened to embarrassing shouting matches between franchise owners and company executives, and I have seen classically quiet standoffs and even a few mature discussions. The exciting thing about an association meeting was that I never knew what to expect.

There were many reasons for the hostility between franchise owners and the parent company. Probably the most common complaints were menu and product limitations. Can you imagine investing hundreds of thousands of dollars, working twenty hours a day, and having no authority to add a customer-requested item to your menu? Franchise owners could not even change catsup brands without permission.

Just to make sure franchise owners did not make unauthorized changes,

I made monthly visits and reported any continual irregularities to the vice-president and staff attorney. At the same time, I would do courtesy health, fire, equipment, safety, and accounting inspections. Often I would spend two days sneaking around the franchise restaurant trying to recruit employee informants and catch the franchise owner doing something wrong.

A popular cause for unrest among franchise owners was the evolution of franchise contracts. When our company first began to offer franchises, the contracts were often flexible and more favorable for the franchise owners. As the company gained experience with franchising and franchise owners, the contracts predictably became very rigid, legalistic, and more favorable to the parent company (sometimes called a "sweetheart" contract). That produced a large, diverse group of franchise owners with just as many varieties of contracts.

Some of my franchise owners, for example, were allowed to do their own local store marketing (individual unit advertising controlled by the franchise owner) while others had to pay a fixed percentage of their gross revenue or a regional allocation in return for regional or national advertising (controlled by the marketing department at company headquarters). Of course, the most obvious difference in franchise contracts is their cost. The old "granddaddy" franchises were relatively inexpensive compared to later generations .

Another tender issue facing the franchise owners and the parent company is the use of required products from the commissary. The commissary was a thriving profit center for the company. All the company-owned units had to purchase all their supplies through the commissary even if they were less expensive through local sources. The reason was that a single source of profit from the commissary was easier to manage than slightly increased profits from hundreds of company units. The franchise owners were "encouraged" to use the commissary because it was the only reliable source of "approved" products. Some franchise owners had units thousands of miles from the commissary. Their monthly deliveries made storage expensive and ordering difficult.

One distant group of franchise owners decided to make its own hamburger sauce instead of buying it from the commissary. The hamburger sauce must have been a high-profit item for the commissary because the company immediately charged the group with breach of contract. Judging from the behavior of the top company executives, I could tell which ones were getting the biggest cuts from the commissary.

The last thing I would like to mention is the training program offered to new franchise owners. After the prospective franchise owner signed all the contracts, deposited his cash and security agreements, and leased or purchased the land, building, and equipment, he was ready to start training. Six weeks before the unit's opening, the franchise owner and his key employees were invited to company headquarters for intensive training.

We had a full-time training manager and training staff. They could actually work miracles, training a franchise owner with no previous foodservice experience in six weeks. Many of our franchise owners were successful business people, and it was fun to watch them hopping around on a slick, quarry tile floor in the middle of a lunch rush. I always watched from a distance so I would not get sprayed with imitation ice cream from a whirling milk shake machine or become the target of four giant drinks. The trainees dressed in neat management uniforms, but within a few hours their paper hats were on sideways, their polyester slacks were snagged, their name badges had been ripped off and taped back on upside down, their shoes were corroded, and their ties looked like potato chips dipped in sour cream.

Training restaurants are like bumper car concessions. Some franchise owners did not seem to mind the confusion and hard work. Others would stay a few days and then back out of the contract. Still others remained the entire six weeks, but were continually uncooperative. We had several franchise owners who refused to wear a paper hat, and one refused to wear the management uniform. Occasionally the trainers would suggest that a franchise owner consider going into another line of work. Sometimes an owner would disappear and we would never see him again.

To sum up the whole topic of franchising, it's both good and bad for the company (franchisor) and for the franchise owner (franchisee). Franchising is a quick and effective way to expand a company without borrowing money or using internal profits. On the other hand, the franchisor receives demanding and often inexperienced partners in return. The franchisee has the possibility of making a fortune, depending on the company's image and his own wherewithal. But the franchise fee is usually expensive, and landlords charge high rents for owners of first-class franchises.

I have a friend who bought a well-known doughnut franchise. He and his wife worked seven days a week, twelve hours a day, for two years. I never saw them except when they were behind the counter with flour in their hair and raspberry filling on their shirts. Both of them developed gigantic shoulders and arms from rolling the dough. They also developed pot bellies from a lack of any other exercise. Their faces were pasty, with black rings around their eyes. They went broke. The franchisor took back their franchise, their meager savings, their house, and their car. My friend seemed grateful. He said, "That franchise was like having a terminal illness."

There are many successes, however. Another friend bought a franchise territory from one of the nation's largest hamburger chains. He started in the early 1960s with money borrowed on the equity on his house. He had one unit and worked seven days a week, twelve hours a day, for three years. Then he built a second unit and hired a general manager. Later he added more units, until he had twenty restaurants, twenty managers, three district managers, and a vice-president of operations. He now lives in the nicest house in the nicest part of town.

I often eat lunch at a nearby yogurt shop. The franchisee recently said, "If it weren't for my wife, I'd never be able to spend all the money I make." Sometimes we walk through his parking lot and count empty yogurt cups tossed on the pavement. He says, "Each of those cups represents two dollars in my pocket." I think those cups could arouse the entrepreneurial spirit in all of us.

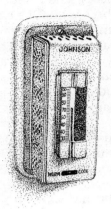

5

Your Landlord

What You Should Know about Leases and Leashes

When Renee and I bought our first two restaurants, we also purchased the land and buildings. We really never thought much about landlords. Our third restaurant was in a large building that we shared with several other tenants. Our landlord also had a business there. The first time we met him, he said, "We'll get along just fine. I'm very fair. Just trust me." It did not take long for us to realize the full meaning of his words.

Before we could buy our third restaurant, we had to negotiate a new lease or get the existing lease transferred. The sellers suggested we keep the same lease because it contained several favorable clauses for the restaurant. For example, it required the landlord to provide heat, air-conditioning, and garbage service. The major disadvantage of the existing lease was that it expired in three years. We decided to negotiate a longer lease so we would not be at the mercy of the landlord and deadly rent increases just when we really got the business going.

The sellers did not think we should renegotiate the lease, because we might lose the favorable clauses in the process. In fact, they did not even think we should meet with the landlord to discuss anything. It quickly became clear that the sellers and landlord were not the best of friends. According to the sellers, the landlord did not do anything to maintain the building. According to the landlord, the sellers always paid the rent late. Renee and I were determined to make friends with the landlord before we bought the restaurant.

We had lunch with the landlord and his wife to discuss the lease. They were friendly but somewhat hesitant about extending the life of the lease beyond three years. We explained how important it was to have a longer lease when investing a large sum of money in a business. The lease was one of the most valuable assets. They finally agreed, and we signed a new lease for twelve years, with all the favorable clauses left intact. We talked quite a while after lunch, and the landlord said, "The real reason we agreed to extend the lease is to get rid of those people who own the restaurant now." I was thinking how those same people were probably selling it just to get rid of the landlord.

The day we transferred possession of the restaurant, the landlord came marching in, shouting and waving his arms. He walked up to the seller and stuck a rent check in his face. "This bounced, and I just called my lawyer to sue you. And I want you to know that I'm glad you're leaving." The seller just backed away until the landlord left and then said to me, "He deserved it." I did not want to think about the incident and hoped it was an isolated personality conflict.

Renee and I quickly forgot about the first day and devoted ourselves to running the restaurant. We were open for breakfast, lunch, and dinner, and worked all three shifts ourselves. None of the other tenants were open at night; consequently, the lighting in the halls and at the entrances was not very good. One morning the landlord came in for coffee and offered to add more lights. He said it might encourage the other tenants to stay open later too. We were extremely pleased because several of our customers had complained about the dark and dangerous stairs.

Two days later a worker started drilling into cement walls and ceilings. After two weeks of noise, dust, and swearing, the worker finished hanging three secondhand chandeliers. None of them matched, and they definitely did not complement the rest of the building.

The landlord came in the next morning carrying a bag full of fifteen-watt light bulbs. Each chandelier had seven sockets, and he wanted to conserve electricity. Some of the sockets were dead, and the working sockets would not even cast a shadow with the tiny light bulbs. He eventually started putting in a variety of ugly bulbs because they happened to be on sale. I had finally discovered what the seller meant when he said, "He deserved it."

One day the meter reader informed me that I was paying the electricity for the three new chandeliers in the halls. We asked him to hook them up to the landlord's common-area meter. He did, and the landlord never mentioned the incident—but he never replaced another bulb in those chandeliers.

Light bulbs became a big issue because the landlord seldom replaced them, and there were hundreds throughout the common areas. We were the only tenants with a written lease, and it specified that the landlord would maintain those areas. The other tenants were powerless to demand any sort of upkeep. I asked the landlord if I could purchase and replace light bulbs and subtract the cost from our lease payments. He was not interested until I told him that he would not have to worry about light bulbs anymore and I would not charge him for my labor. He finally agreed. I did not tell him my lawyer had already advised me to go ahead and charge him for everything if he refused.

I changed all the bulbs to a higher wattage and fixed the dead sockets myself. Some months I would spend one hundred dollars on bulbs and fluorescent tubes. After a while the other tenants would come to me and "borrow" bulbs for their personal use. I would even catch the landlord sneaking around and stealing his own light bulbs from the common area. The light bulb business turned out to be time-consuming, and a restaurant owner has little time to spare. But it probably prevented a long and costly legal battle.

As I mentioned, the lease required the landlord to provide the restaurant with heat. Shortly after we took possession, the landlord removed our thermostat. He had decided to control the heat in the entire building with one central thermostat located in the hall. We felt it was extremely unfair because anybody walking down the hall could adjust it. We managed until winter approached, and then some of the tenants wanted less heat while our customers wanted more. The tenants finally complained to the landlord.

The next day the landlord replaced the old thermostat with a new one that locked, and set the temperature at sixty-eight degrees. It took only a few minutes before our customers started complaining again about how cold it was in our restaurant.

I asked the landlord for a key to the thermostat, but he refused and said his lawyer suggested sixty-eight degrees as both economical and fair. I knew this attitude of being fair quickly was going to put me out of business. That night a friend helped me break into the thermostat. We readjusted it to seventy-two degrees and bent the needle so it would read sixty-eight degrees. The landlord became suspicious when I stopped complaining and a few of the other tenants commented that it was too warm in the building. I soon discovered the thermostat had been lowered to sixty-six degrees. Again my friend and I sneaked into the hall one night and bent the needle even further. But then our customers complained of too much heat. We simply needed a thermostat of our own, and the landlord was not going to oblige unless we wanted to fight it out in court.

I was complaining to a shop owner across the hall one day when he asked if I knew about the old thermostat behind a painting in his office. He said it might still work if we connected the wires. That is exactly what we did, and it overrode the landlord's whole system. The shop owner gave me a key so we could adjust the thermostat when he was out. The landlord never found out about the secret thermostat. I smiled when he would comment, "The heat seems to have a mind of its own."

Needless to say, we used plenty of heat that winter, and the landlord raised everyone's rent to cover the added costs, plus a little extra. He raised everyone's—except ours, because we had a fixed lease. Renee and I felt guilty about the rent increase for the shop owner who had the secret thermostat. But he did not mind and enjoyed the intrigue.

Obviously our landlord was a strange person. One day he would try to be our best friend and the next he would be our worst enemy. He and his wife invited us to dinner one evening. We probably were strange ourselves for accepting the invitation. It turned out to be very enjoyable, except for the landlord's driving. He was one of those people who turns around and looks at you sitting in the back seat while he is driving. He used to wreck his car almost every month. He even wrecked the loaners.

Once he got mad at a tenant for not paying rent on time and he put a dead rat in the tenant's window to scare customers. I asked him to fix a handrail one day, and he got so mad that he started screaming and running around in circles. He did not speak to me for almost a month, until I apologized. I did not apologize for anything in particular, just everything in general. He fixed the handrail.

The cost of our summer air-conditioning, provided in the lease, also gave the landlord headaches. The building had both central air-conditioning and a network of old swamp coolers. In the summer we would need everything going to keep it cool because of the open passage to our outdoor patio. The central air-conditioning had a separate thermostat, which the landlord kept locked. I tried forcing the cover off one day to turn it on and "accidentally" broke it instead. I told the landlord I had seen some teenagers roaming the building that day. He put a new locked cover on the thermostat the following week.

I was losing my patience with the landlord and spending far too much time on temperature control. I needed to do something clever. Since this thermostat was the round type, I could loosen the whole unit, twist it a half inch, and tighten it back on the wall without anyone noticing. I did this, and it kept the building five degrees cooler all summer; I had tilted the mercury switch so it made the thermostat always think it was five degrees warmer than it actually was.

A month after that minor adjustment, the landlord wanted to raise everyone's rent again after he saw his utility bill. The tenants flatly refused and threatened to move out. They told him, "You won't find anyone else who'll pay this kind of rent. Anyway, you owe us a few cool summers." The landlord backed down and tried a different approach. He painted the roof a reflective color and put in an attic fan. We also got a new front door because the old one did not close tightly. All these things lowered his next utility bill a little but not enough.

Then the landlord started coming into the building late at night and turning off all the circuit breakers for the central air-conditioning and swamp coolers. In the morning it would be almost ninety degrees in the building. If we turned on all the breakers as soon as we got there at 6:00 A.M. it would take almost four hours to cool it down to seventy-five degrees. I asked the landlord to leave the circuit breakers on and taped a note to the breaker panel. The note was gone the next morning and the breakers were off. I even came back to the restaurant a few times in the middle of the night just to turn them back on.

We did not quite know how to solve that particular problem with our landlord, until someone told us he was afraid of the dark. The next day my friend with the secret thermostat and I asked all the tenants to turn off their night lights. We also disconnected the wall switches near the back door, where the landlord usually came into the building at night. The next morning the breakers were on and the back door was unlocked. We guessed the landlord had gotten so nervous he forgot to lock it. Later that day he asked if we knew what had happened to all the night lights. We said, "Yes, we all turned them off to save electricity."

Our landlord was always remodeling his office. Instead of giving his old furniture to charity, he would put it in our common areas. After a while, our common areas began to look like used-furniture stores on bargain day. We asked him to haul it away, but he said it was his building and he liked it there. People from off the street started sitting in our common areas and even brought picnics. It was cool inside, and they sometimes stayed all afternoon. Their kids would run up and down the halls and play on the carpet. It was like a city park. The transients would come into our restaurant begging for money. They never asked for food. We would tell them to go down the hall and ask the landlord.

It got so bad we finally called the fire marshal, and he ordered all the furniture removed because the building had exceeded its maximum occupancy. While he was still there, I pointed out a locked side door leading to the parking lot. The landlord stubbornly refused to unlock the door during the day, and it was an inconvenience for our customers. The fire marshal ordered the door unlocked during business hours and fined the landlord.

Our landlord was so cheap he refused to clean the carpets in the common areas. Every month he would have the carpet in his office and in a small patch directly outside his door cleaned. It made the entire common area look even worse next to the landlord's spot of clean carpet. When we asked him to have it cleaned, he would reply, "Just trust me." One day he felt generous and offered to rent a carpet-cleaning machine if I would do the work. My patience came to an end. I waited until the landlord was out of the building, then hired a carpet-cleaning service. I instructed the workers to steam-clean all the common areas except the patch outside the landlord's door. They said it was the most disgusting carpet they had ever seen, but it looked beautiful when they finished, with the exception of the dirty patch right outside the landlord's door.

When the landlord returned, he asked my friend across the hall with the secret thermostat who had cleaned the carpets. My friend told him about the cleaning service that I had arranged and paid for. The landlord was smiling as he shook my hand and thanked me for having the carpets cleaned. I told him the carpet service skipped the area outside his door because it was beginning to wear out from too much cleaning.

The next week was the first of the month, and our lease payment was due. I personally went to the landlord's office with our check. Actually, I had two checks. I handed him the first and waited for his response. "Where's the rest of the money," he demanded. I said, "I subtracted the cost of the carpet cleaning from the payment and will send you the receipt for your records." The landlord stood up and croaked, "You can't do that." I reminded him of line ninety-two of our lease, requiring him to maintain the common areas.

"I won't accept this check, and you'll be hearing from my lawyer." Trying to be as annoyingly calm as I possibly could, I took back the first check and handed him the second. It was written for even a lesser amount. I explained how I had subtracted an additional amount for my own time and labor. Then I said, "Which check do you want?" The landlord jerked the first check out of my hand and threw the other on the desk in front of me.

I called the bank later that day to see if he had cashed the check. He had, which meant he had accepted payment and probably would not file suit. The very next day he had the dirty patch of carpet cleaned outside his door. It really was beginning to look threadbare.

I now understood why the previous owner of our restaurant never sent his lease payments on time. Every month they would wait until the landlord threatened foreclosure before dropping his check into a remote mailbox with limited collection service. They even purchased a postage machine so they could give the envelope a proper date but drop it in the mail a week or two later.

Always read leases carefully. Avoid a lease that has an automatic default or a short grace period, for late payments. Grace periods are normally ten days but can begin when the default occurs, when the default notice is postmarked, or when you receive your notice. Remember that some landlords have their own postage machines with adjustable dates. If you are unable to correct a default within the grace period, ask your landlord for an extension in writing or call your lawyer for a temporary restraining order.

Renee and I often thought about using our ten-day grace period when it came time for the monthly lease payment, but we decided it would not accomplish anything significant. It was more important for us to maintain a solid credit record and save our energy for issues like carpet cleaning.

One of the most exciting things about our lease was the maintenance of the common rest rooms. The lease stipulated that the landlord would maintain the rest rooms in good working order according to county health codes. We did not think much about it until a week after we took possession of the restaurant.

Two tiny rest rooms handled all the tenants, all our customers, and all our employees. Besides the continual stream of people from our own building, other nearby businesses told their customers to use our rest rooms. We could not believe what we had done: we had leased a public rest room. Our landlord had his own private rest room. We tried sending some of our customers down to his office, but he always claimed the facility was out of order.

The rest rooms had permanent lines of people waiting to use them. Paper products lasted only about an hour before they needed restocking. And I bet you can guess how well the landlord maintained them!

Our landlord never went into those rest rooms. The other tenants did not clean them either, so why should we worry? The first week our customers complained about no toilet paper, no soap, no towels, and the sickening odor.

Then the health inspector called. His office had received several complaints from angry customers. I told him he would have to speak with the landlord because the rest rooms were his responsibility. An hour later the health inspector called again and sympathetically informed us it was our responsibility to keep the rest rooms cleaned and stocked. Otherwise, he would have to close us down. Since we were the only restaurant in the building, we were the only tenants required to have rest rooms.

I called our lawyer and asked how much I could deduct from the monthly lease payments for rest-room maintenance. He suggested I deduct no more than the amount of one monthly payment over the next year. That meant I could not charge for my time and labor. I compromised again and told the landlord I would maintain the rest rooms if I could deduct the cost of supplies from our lease payment. He agreed and seemed satisfied.

Rest-room maintenance became a large part of our lives. Several times a day Renee and I had to clean and stock them. We also had to order and store cases of toilet paper, paper towels, hand soap, and disinfectant. We tried delegating rest-room maintenance to our employees, but they complained so much it was not worth it. A burned-out light bulb in the rest room would send a dozen people hurrying into our restaurant during a lunch rush, all asking us to replace it immediately. Several times a week I would fight my way through the lines of people, carrying my plumber's helper. If we did not immediately unplug a toilet, people would continue using it, after it overflowed.

We were constantly angry at the people using the rest rooms, especially if they were not our customers. The biggest mistake we made was keeping them too clean. We got a reputation in town for having the cleanest public rest rooms. Business owners from three blocks away would send their customers to our building to use the facilities.

I found out the other business owners were reducing their insurance premiums by telling their customers they did not have a rest room. I suppose the insurance companies thought it would be less risky if the customers did not have to walk through crowded and dangerous storerooms to their facilities. Sometimes Renee would ask people waiting in line outside our rest rooms who was recommending us. She discovered it was the pizza parlor owner across the street.

Before long we were spending more time maintaining the rest rooms than operating the restaurant. Worst yet, we were constantly angry about the whole thing. Just when we would start to forget about the rest rooms, someone would come into the restaurant and tell us about the disposable diaper stopping up the toilet. Once I made the mistake of buying two-ply tissue. It plugged up all the sewer lines in the building.

One day, in a fit of temper, I put padlocks on the rest-room doors. It was wonderful watching all the people come in from outside to find the doors locked. It was especially wonderful watching the ones who obviously were in a hurry. We let our customers and the other tenants borrow the key. The locked rest rooms got just as filthy just as quickly, and keeping track of the key was a full-time job. Our customers began propping the doors open with a waste bucket, and once there was a line it did not matter anyway. We also learned that people do not like locked rest rooms and tend to leave disgusting little reminders of their disapproval.

I took down the rest-room signs and replaced them with Keep Out and Office signs. I thought the confusing signs would discourage most of the street people. We told our customers that Keep Out was for men and Office was for women. The street people just ignored the new signs, but our customers would forget the code and have to come back to the restaurant. It was interesting to watch our customers react to the signs. Keep Out really made the men nervous. On the other hand, street people would bounce into our restaurant and tell us the Office was out of toilet paper.

I even tried turning off the electricity into the rest rooms and taping Out of Order signs on the doors. That was another mistake because one lady went in anyway and fell. It was dark inside and she missed the seat. She promised she would not sue us if I turned the lights on. That is exactly what I did, and I found that some disgusting person had missed the seat in the men's room, too.

We even had someone who did threaten to sue us over those stupid rest rooms. There happened to be a small hole in the door of the men's room. One day a nicely dressed businessman bitterly complained to Renee that someone had been watching him through the hole. He did not threaten us with a lawsuit until Renee asked, "What were you doing in there that's making you so upset?" Luckily we never heard from him or his lawyer. We certainly did not want to call our lawyer again. He already recognized our voices right away.

We knew we would have to do something clever with the rest-room situation after we decided to sell the restaurant. They needed paint and new sinks, and one needed a new toilet. We also needed to discourage street people permanently from using them. My friend with the secret thermostat and I made a plan. First we asked the landlord if he would paint the rest rooms. He said, "Absolutely not." So we offered to paint them for the cost of the paint, and he agreed. We bought the best-quality paint and deducted it from our lease payment. After giving the rest rooms two coats, we still had enough paint left over to do my friend's shop.

Next we made an anonymous call to the health department and complained about our own rest-room sinks because they did not have any hot water. The inspector was waiting for us the next morning. He said, "We got a complaint about your rest rooms not having any hot water." I answered, "We sure hope the landlord does something about the sinks when he fixes the hot water. They're so pitted we can't keep them clean." That afternoon we had sparkling new sinks with hot water.

We wanted to replace the men's toilet, because it took almost two hours to fill up when the water pressure was low in the summer. I was tired of hauling water in gallon jugs from the restaurant to fill the tank every time someone flushed it. I knew the landlord had a storeroom directly under the men's room. A few years earlier the toilet had overflown, ruining some of his supplies, and the landlord had immediately hired a plumber.

I helped that old toilet get stuck again one evening. The water poured into his storeroom all night. A plumber installed a new toilet and pressure regulator early the next morning. We all conveyed our sincere sympathy to the landlord.

The final stage of our rest-room plan was to discourage people from using them. Nothing had worked up to that point. Then I remembered that when I was a manager trainee in a fast-food restaurant, gangs would come in to use the facilities and often end up fighting. My assistant manager told me to use ammonia. (At first I thought she meant in their eyes.) We would mop the rest-room floors with straight ammonia every hour. The gangs soon found another all-night rest room. I decided to do the same thing again. The entire building smelled like ammonia for a month, but the street people eventually found another place to go.

The battle of the rest rooms was well worth the effort. When we put our restaurant up for sale, the first place our buyers inspected was the rest rooms.

We did not bother boring them with the details and history of those two tiny rooms.

A common type of lease is the triple net. It simply means the tenant is responsible for the insurance, the taxes, and the net payments to the landlord. Our lease required the landlord to pay the insurance and taxes on the building, even though we carried our own insurance and paid our own taxes on the business. The lease stated that if the cost of the landlord's taxes and insurance increased, he could pass the cost on to us and, of course, the other tenants. He complained daily about the skyrocketing insurance premiums and the soaring property taxes. He said, "I regret raising your rent, but it's just costing me too much of my own money. Trust me." He said he was sorry, but everyone, including us, would have to pay an extra hundred dollars a month.

My friend and I asked him for copies of his insurance and tax statements for the past three years. We wanted to compare his present costs with his past costs and determine the actual percentage increase. He did not like our questioning his calculations. He reminded all of us, "Just trust me." We stuck together and refused to pay the extra hundred dollars until he gave us the statements.

His property taxes had remained the same for the three-year period, but we could not decipher the insurance rates. I took them to my own insurance broker. She found the premium had indeed increased about one hundred dollars a month, but for the entire building. She calculated our share of the increase, according to gross leased area, at $3.50 a month. We were eager to tell the landlord what he already knew. Renee and I also told our insurance broker to charge us for her services. Her fee was deducted from our next lease payment. We were finally starting to learn about leases and leashes.

I want to mention a few other important clauses in our lease. One was a leasehold improvement clause, which basically said that everything we nailed to the floor, walls, or ceiling belonged to the landlord. He would sit in our restaurant and admire all the paintings hanging on the walls because he thought they had become his property. We got nervous about his proprietary attitude and called our lawyer. He told us not to worry. The courts usually interpret the clause as meaning that additions and improvements to the building become the property of the landlord if their eventual removal would damage or alter the original structure. All we had to do was plug holes and paint after we removed our things.

Renee made a point of telling the other tenants what our lawyer had said. We got together and told the landlord we were all going to move out at the same time. Then we were going to call the building inspector and tell him that the building was unsafe because the floors, walls, and ceilings were nothing but plugs and paint.

Another clause in our lease required the landlord to provide garbage pickup for the building. At first he had a dozen old, metal trash cans behind the building. In the summer the smell caused the neighbors to complain constantly. They also complained that their own dogs were bringing home our trash. Our employees even complained about the trash cans because of the smell, the bees, and the snarling dogs. Our landlord finally poured a cement slab and rented a dumpster with a lid from the garbage company.

Our restaurant was responsible for most of the garbage that went into the dumpster. As the months passed, the landlord's dumpster fee began increasing because we were getting busier and generating more garbage. Our lease prevented the landlord from transferring the increase to us, and he became obsessed with our garbage.

A day after it had been emptied, I noticed our dumpster was full of garbage from another restaurant down the street. Our landlord had rented a portion of the dumpster to help offset the increasing costs. He said, "With the money I get from the other restaurant, I end up paying less than I did before with just the old trash cans." Renee and I considered offering to help pay for the garbage service, but our lease payments were already too high.

It was not long before the dumpster was always overflowing with rotting garbage from both restaurants. The garbage was piled so high that the lids would not close, and dogs would actually jump five feet up into the dumpster and guard it all day. When we tried to throw in our garbage, it would just slide off onto the ground—assuming the dogs and yellow jackets would let us get close enough.

The other restaurant had its name and logo printed on napkins and placemats. I began searching through the garbage with a stick pulling out all these items. Then I would spread them around our parking lot, especially near the door used by the landlord. I would also toss a few into the yards of the neighbors. It was not long before we were the only restaurant using the dumpster.

One thing you must do if you have a dumpster is steam-clean it every few months, especially in the summer. Our landlord was not interested in having the dumpster cleaned because the garbage company charged a fee. Once a month in the summer we would make an anonymous call to the health department and complain about the smell and the swarms of blue-green flies nesting in the dumpster. We would tell the landlord, "If the neighbors would mind their own business, you wouldn't have to keep that dumpster so clean."

The last clause I should mention was the one dealing with pest control. It required the landlord to contract with a professional exterminator. We never saw an exterminator. The landlord would say, "Let nature take its course. Survival of the fittest." Nature did take its course, and our building became infested with fit cockroaches. I would spray poison on the floor along the walls, and it would chase the cockroaches across the hall into my friend's shop or down the hall into one of the other businesses.

Whoever got the cockroaches would spray and send them scampering back to our restaurant. We chased cockroaches around the building until we thought of another plan. We all sprayed at the same time, leaving the landlord's office the only place free of pesticide. One morning he walked into his office, turned on the lights, and saw thousands of cockroaches scatter for cover. All of us kept spraying regularly for another week, until we got notices explaining the schedule of our new professional exterminator.

As you can see, the lease itself is just the beginning. The heart of the matter is how well you can establish a working relationship with your landlord and how well you can compromise. If you are thinking about signing a lease, by all means consult a lawyer. Don't be afraid to interview the current and past tenants of a potential landlord. Also remember that a good landlord can sell the property to a bad landlord. Finally, smile the next time you hear a landlord mutter, "Just trust me."

6

Systems Management
How to Make a Faster Tuna Sandwich

You probably recognize the term *systems management*. It is very popular in management today and even more popular in management textbooks. Everyone has a tendency to use the term rather loosely. If you were to ask a hospitality executive the meaning of the term, you would probably get a reply such as "It's the only viable approach we have to manage our resources and measure our results." If you were to ask a hospitality professor to explain the term you might hear, "Of course, systems management is the interaction of the microenvironment and macroenvironment with the dynamic evolution of proactive management objectives." The truth is that most hospitality professors put us to sleep with all their talk about systems management, and many hospitality executives simply should be put to sleep.

I recently boiled down a few of these systems management books. They all said the same thing in the final analysis: "Systems management is nothing but a manager's way of coping with change." The textbooks ask you to accept, trust, and incorporate change into your activities. The interesting twist is that systems, by their nature, tend to isolate themselves from change.

The best definition I have ever heard for systems management came from my first boss, Joe. He would say, "Mikey, you've gotta have a system for everything in the restaurant business or you just won't make it." I was fourteen when I started using systems management, and I always get a kick out of high-powered executives and high-thinking scholars who treat it as their new crystal ball.

I developed my first system when I was a dishwasher. Instead of sending an assortment of dishes through the dish machine, I would sort and stack high piles of dirty dishes around it. Then I would rack and wash only one type of dish at a time. It was much faster, and it kept all the loaded bus trays off the floor.

Frequently, large dried chunks of food would be stuck to the clean dishes. I learned quickly that the intense heat of the final rinse phase made these miniature meals brittle and easily removable with a fingernail.

Dishwashing personnel often take more than their share of abuse. My system for self-defense was to keep the floor of the dish room extremely wet and my shirt and apron covered with disgusting stains. That discouraged the slippery-shoed servers and bus help from coming into the dish room demanding more clean dishes. My messy shirt and apron usually prevented the older and more dangerous cooks from grabbing my shirt, backing me up against the wall, and threatening me with butcher knives unless I returned their favorite pots.

I also had an effective system for revenge. For the arrogant bus help, I sent all the dinner knives through the dish machine twice. Our dinner knives were heavy and retained the heat. After two final rinses, the knives became red-hot. I would save all the knives until the bus help ran out, and they would have to set all the tables at once with hot knives, burning their fingers.

For the servers, I would heat up their cold salad plates in the final rinse and leave a puddle of water in each coffee cup's saucer as I stacked them. For the ill-tempered cooks, I would stack the stainless steel insert pans when they were still hot and wet. It created a vacuum when they cooled, and they became almost impossible to pry apart. I also resorted to hiding favorite pots and occasionally tossing one out if a cook continually burned the bottom.

A common unwritten system in the restaurant business is for servers to take only one order at a time and deliver it to the kitchen before taking another. This system becomes seriously inconvenient because customers often arrive in waves. When this happens, servers take as many orders as possible and give them to the kitchen all at once. This is called "sandbagging," and it will generate loud obscenities from the kitchen staff. The cooks have a retaliatory system that generates equally loud obscenities and amusing body language from the servers. They cook all the orders so they come up at exactly the same time. If a server has orders for three or four tables come up at once, only the first table will receive hot food. The other orders are at the mercy of the heat lamps.

Servers also develop a habit of holding onto their orders, instead of giving them to the cooks, so they have time to serve their customers soup and salad before the entrees. This system is especially amenable to orders that are easy and quick to cook. But when the server finally places these orders with the kitchen, the cooks may be too busy to give them priority. Even if the cooks are not busy, they may purposely delay the orders just to badger the servers.

I experienced these waves of customers when I worked as a cook in Joe's large open kitchen. Between orders, we would sit on the work tables, drink coffee, and stare at the customers. It was great fun because what we were really saying to the customers with our eyes was "We're sitting exactly on the spot where your food is going to be trimmed, pounded, breaded, sliced, and assembled."

After the dining room was completely full, the orders would start coming into the kitchen. It would take the servers about thirty minutes to deliver all two hundred orders to the kitchen. During that time we continued to sit on the tables, smiling at the customers, and looking totally relaxed. That confused and angered the customers because they wondered why we were not working frantically. It also made the servers angry because they knew what we were going to do. After all the orders were in, the head cook would place a number on each guest check or group of checks. That number indicated which orders we would cook first, second, and so forth. The system was remarkable, and so was the head cook. Everyone in the restaurant was served very quickly and almost simultaneously. If we tried to serve everyone on a first-come, first-served basis, we would have added long hours to our cooking time. We called our system the "waitress killer."

Joe also taught me the value of the station system, which meant that every person was assigned a station with specific responsibilities. Using the station system was always a treat because it involved maximum staffing and the time passed very quickly. We worked stations on Friday and Saturday evenings. Each server was assigned a certain portion of the dining room. Each bartender was responsible for a particular section of the bar. Each cook was responsible for certain food items.

How fast the customers were seated and what they ordered determined if we were going to be busy. Some evenings, customers would order nothing but steaks and seafood. That slowed down the kitchen because the customers stayed longer at the tables. Other times they would order just pasta and stay long enough to empty the Parmesan cheese bowl and stain the tablecloth.

Working stations was easy because you never had to worry about coordinating orders, except the head cook. He simply told us when to start cooking a particular menu item so the food for an entire table would come up at approximately the same time.

For the cooks, the secret to the work station system was the day of the month. On paydays near the middle and end of the month, I asked for the pasta or pizza stations. On those days customers had more money and did not order the inexpensive items. Other times, when customers were predictably short of money, I always wanted the seafood station.

At sixteen I became head cook. I had a knack for coordinating the orders and could get the food out even faster than Joe. I looked young for my age, and it must have been worrisome for customers to walk into an expensive restaurant to find a high school kid sitting on the work table, telling four older cooks when to flame the veal and how much fresh dill to use in the scallops.

Have you ever wondered what kitchens used before microwave ovens? We had a system for defrosting things that was almost as fast. It was the boiling pots of water used to heat precooked pasta. We precooked our pasta to the *al dente* stage, which meant it was still a little tough. Then we would drain and refrigerate it until we got an order. It took only a few seconds in boiling water to reheat the pasta.

We also boiled fresh chicken in the pasta water before frying it. The chicken fat helped keep the pasta from sticking together. Our frozen lobster tails were tossed into the same water for five minutes before we baked them in the oven. I have even boiled frozen steaks before putting them on the broiler. I didn't have to worry about changing the water very often because the pasta soaked up the fishy flavors. This may be of some interest to readers who are strict vegetarians.

The pasta water also was our system for heating baby bottles. We would let the bottle sink to the bottom and stay there for a few moments. Then the four cooks would check the temperature by pumping the nipple onto their hairy arms.

Our system for closing that crazy kitchen is an interesting story. We were instructed by Joe not to close before 11:00 P.M. At 10:30 we would put the Closed sign in the window, but customers just ignored it and came in anyway. After years of having to cook for a rush of drunken customers who came in just minutes before closing, we finally had an idea. One evening when Joe was gone, we reversed the switches on the outside lights. We would turn them off at 10:30, but the switches appeared to be on. That worked for a few days, until we turned them off one evening with Joe standing outside.

We finally just started closing the kitchen at 10:30 anyway and told the servers they could serve anything they could find. I will probably never have another job as secure as that one.

When I was in the fast-food business, one of the first things we learned was the difference between cooking-to-order and cooking ahead. These two systems were the basics of fast-food operation. We used the cooking-to-order system during slow periods. Imagine pulling up to a drive-through speaker box at about three o'clock in the afternoon. You wanted to avoid the lunch rush so you waited until everything quieted down. You place your order, and then you are instructed to pull forward to the window. Whether you know it or not, your food will be subjected to the cooking-to-order system.

The cooking-to-order system really means everything in the kitchen has been returned to the freezer or refrigerator. It also means that most of the employees have gone home. The remaining employees are probably taking their afternoon naps. Do not be alarmed. There are always one or two employees ready to cook an order especially for you. These afternoon employees often are assigned this particular shift because they are not fast enough to work the lunch and dinner rushes. They are also prone to making mistakes, such as forgetting your order. Make sure to ask for your change from afternoon employees.

These employees are mostly hired to clean the toilets, garbage area, and parking lot. In fact, they might cook your order and pour your drinks between cleaning the men's and ladies' rest rooms. I always enjoyed working with these afternoon employees because of their creativity. This same creativity frequently landed them in jail, and I would have to hire others, usually their friends. I estimate the average afternoon employee usually stays for about a month before disappearing.

Cooking-to-order, by definition, is much more time-consuming than cooking ahead. That is why you will probably turn off your motor after waiting twenty minutes for a fillet-of-fish sandwich and a diet soda. The afternoon employees are never in a hurry. They have learned from experience just to bide their time. First they will chip off a frozen fillet of fish from an unidentifiable mass that has been thawed and refrozen a dozen times. Then they will plop the square of fish into a cold fryer. After noticing the fish did not bubble and fizz in the grease, they will turn the knob and begin reheating the fryer while your fish is soaking up all those nasty fats.

Next they will toast your bun on a beautifully clean grill. After the lunch rush someone always "bricks" the grill (using a black, porous, and lightweight piece of processed pumice stone the size and shape of a brick) or uses a liquid cleaner. Not only does this make the grill nice and shiny, but also it leaves a chemical or gritty residue. The afternoon employee will not just place your bun on the grill surface, he will also use it to wipe and polish the grill by making a series of circular motions.

Next the afternoon employee will dress your bun. The tartar sauce will not chill the fish sandwich, because it has been sitting next to the hot grill since morning. The lettuce container is probably empty, so the afternoon employee might fish out of the garbage can some discarded outer leaves. These outer lettuce leaves also have tough white spines, brown by now, making your afternoon cooked-to-order sandwich lumpy and difficult to slide into a narrow sandwich bag. The afternoon cook will simply place his palm on the assembled sandwich and smash it downward, using a twisting motion, until the tartar sauce squirts out the sides. Then he will take a dirty cleaning rag, gently wipe around the rim of the sandwich, and blot the grease off the top bun. If you ask for a tomato slice from an afternoon employee, you will probably get just the outside skin without any pulp. In the fast-food business we called those tomato slices "old empties."

Now your order is ready and placed into a bag that is so small your hand will not easily fit inside. Your only choice is to dump or shake it out on your lap. This brings us to your diet soda. Even before cooking your fish and toasting your bun, the afternoon employee fills a cup half-full of ice and half-full of flat soda. Diet soda always tastes flat because it does not hold the carbonation as well as regular soda. Then he places it on the ledge of the drive-through window, directly in the sunlight.

As the employee leans out the window and hands you the order, you start your car and think about asking for an extra napkin and catsup packet. You notice the employee's fingernails. Not only are they long and jagged, but there is enough organic matter under them to keep an immunologist busy researching for years.

The second system, cooking ahead, tends to be more exciting but equally disgusting. Almost all fast-food operations vehemently deny cooking ahead. They want you to think their food is absolutely fresh and always cooked to order. But during lunch and dinner rushes, cooking to order becomes impractical. Can you imagine cooking for more than four hundred customers in a two-hour period? Not only do the customers want fast service, they also want their sandwich sliced in eight equal portions, crisp bacon and rare beef, onions sauteed in butter, fries with no salt, fries with no grease, and endless combinations of condiments.

One way of managing this impossible situation is to cook ahead. The assumptions behind this system are (1) the customers can take it or leave it, and (2) your order is ready whenever you are. Cooking ahead in its ideal form provides just enough menu items ready to go without anything getting cold, getting warm, or otherwise losing its quality. This is fairly tricky in fast food because most of the menu items can lose their quality and even their identity within seconds after cooking.

At one extreme, cooking ahead means assembling sandwiches in the morning and selling them cold or reheated for lunch. The other extreme involves complex timing systems such as slowly cooking beef patties in several stages, hoping to sell them before they end up in the chili mix.

Another timing system involves precise holding times, with loud alarms indicating that sandwiches should be tossed away after sitting under heat lamps for so many minutes. When I was a unit manager, sandwiches would slide down chutes and the holding time countdown would begin. Often we would not sell the sandwiches before the alarm, but I certainly did not want to throw away all that food; the cost would be subtracted from my monthly bonus. In situations like that, I would remove all the "dead" sandwiches from the slide and carry them back behind the counter. Then I would send them down the chute a second time, starting the countdown all over again. Sometimes I could restart the same sandwiches three times if they were the larger, more durable ones. The smaller sandwiches had a tendency to dry out faster. I also had to watch the Styrofoam containers. They would melt and weld themselves onto the stainless steel chutes if I reused them too many times.

What happened to the sandwiches that were sent down the chute too many times? One thing we did was give the sandwich a fresh-looking Styrofoam container. First we would take the sandwich apart and add some shredded lettuce. Customers could tell if a sandwich was old by its soggy and wilted lettuce. We also kept a spray bottle of water near the worktable so we could give the bun top a quick squirt to moisten it up. The heat lamps tended to dry and crack the bun tops. Another thing we did was place the sandwich upside down in the container. It stopped the bun's bottom from getting soggier. If all else failed, we removed the beef, fish, bacon, turkey, tomatoes, pickles, and any other items thay could be salvaged. Then we piled the assortment of items next to our grill or worktable and saved them for our afternoon customers.

The cook-ahead system is very effective late at night when drunks use the drive-through window. We used to hold sandwiches and french fries for two or three hours and never have a complaint. We did have to change our system for pulling drinks. During the lunch and dinner rushes, our system was to pack the waxy cups three-quarters full of ice. That reduced the time needed to hold the cup under the dispenser. It worked well during rushes because customers never wanted to get back in line to complain about the shortage of liquid. It also worked at the drive-through during the day because the ice would be melting by the time they would drive away. But the late-night drunks demanded very little ice and lots of liquid. We were more than happy to oblige because we were offsetting that added cost by using old sandwiches. Sometimes we would even save dead sandwiches from lunch and dinner just for our special late-night customers.

The "have it your way" generation really changed fast-food systems. One thing it did was slow down the entire industry. Instead of truly fast food, we now have stand-up cafes and coffee shops. Fast-food companies have had to increase prices greatly because our little darlings will not eat mayonnaise, our spouses will not eat brown lettuce or lettuce treated with chemicals, and we will not eat salt on our six large orders of fries.

Fast-food systems are trying fiercely to accommodate all your fantasies, but the truth is they have probably never used real mayonnaise and never will—it is too expensive and too dangerous to put on sandwiches you keep sending down the chute all afternoon. If you like lettuce, you will have to settle for either brown lettuce or treated lettuce. Those are your only two choices. Remember that you can treat lettuce with small quantities of ascorbic acid (vitamin C). I would be more afraid of the herbicides, pesticides, and synthetic fertilizers. And do not let "organically grown" lettuce fool you. Even if fast-food operations could afford to buy such "natural" lettuce, it still must be grown in dirt with our wonderful water. Also, it is free of pesticides—which makes it the safest place for every imaginable insect to lay its eggs. Do not worry either about salt on your fries; they already contain more fat and wax than candles.

I used to think sliced tomatoes were relatively safe fast-food items, until I saw how they were sliced. Most fast-food tomato slicers consist of six razor-sharp blades at one end of a guillotine. A tomato is placed in the hopper and the operator pushes it through the blades with a quick thrust. Out pop seven perfect tomato slices, assuming the tomato is firm and of the right variety. If not, the guillotine smashes the fruit and sprays seeds and juice all over the operator and the ceiling.

This cute little invention often is used for purposes other than slicing tomatoes. I have seen these slicers used for slicing dead sandwiches and the operator's fingers. Employees cut themselves constantly on these machines, and they are too dangerous to clean completely. So the next time you order tomatoes on your sandwich, think of the guillotine and the afternoon employee with dirty fingernails digging into each juicy slice.

We also devised a few systems for decreasing customer service times. Sometimes those systems decreased customers instead. We trained our employees at the counter never to look a customer in the eye, because it caused him or her to ask questions and waste time. Counter employees learned to talk very mechanically, which effectively intimidates most customers because it is like talking to a robot. Experienced counter employees also learned to speak very quickly. Interestingly enough, if they spoke slowly and clearly, fast-food customers would want them to clarify everything. And customers would usually change their orders, more than once, if it was repeated back to them. That is why we trained our counter employees to rattle off their words rapidly, incoherently, and ending with a very loud, "That'll be $2.85, please." That would cause the other customers standing in line to start shuffling their feet impatiently, which in turn would force the first customer to end the transaction.

When counter employees delivered an order to a customer, they loudly said, "Thank you," then immediately turned their attention to another customer. That made it embarrassing for the first customer to interrupt the second one in case the employee forgot something. Fast-food employees have a saying: "If you want full service you're going to have to pay for it, and we don't offer it here at these prices."

Another system we used in the fast-food industry was a technique for speeding up the drive-through. On Friday and Saturday nights I would hook up a microphone with a long cord to the outside speaker box. When the cars started lining up at about dusk, I would go outside and walk down the line of cars taking their orders. Then I would call them in to the kitchen over the microphone. We could move a car every twenty seconds. The system was very efficient because I placed all the orders in the same sequence and never delayed the transaction with chitchat, indecision, or changes.

The microphone cord stretched for half a block, and it got fairly dangerous out there by myself taking orders at midnight from a bunch of drunks. One night a customer tried to strangle me with the cord because he was being obnoxious and I would not take his order. Another time someone tried to run over me, missed, and hit me with an empty beer bottle instead. After that I hired two security guards to walk with me, and the system worked beautifully.

The rest of the crew got tired of listening to obscene remarks and threats from the Friday and Saturday night customers at the window so they implemented, unknown to me, another system. They called it the weekend surcharge. The customers were usually drunk and tended to have large, expensive orders. When they got the cars moving at a twenty-second clip, the window cashier would add an extra dollar onto the total for each order. It worked splendidly, and they developed a rather sophisticated system for accounting and for distributing the weekend surcharge. The system worked so well that a smaller group of employees started adding on another secret surcharge. When the rest of the night crew found out about the second surcharge, I had to use the security guards to break up a nasty scuffle among my own employees.

As a unit manager, I always enjoyed large bonuses after we introduced the outside microphone system and after I had trained all my counter employees. Then another idea came to me. Does this sound familiar: "Would you like a small, medium, or large soda?" "Would you like cheese on your sandwich?" "Would you like small or large fries?" "Would you like the small or large salad bar?" All these phrases are aimed at increasing sales. The trick is always to end your inquiry with the largest size, because consumer research has proven that customers generally order the last size they hear.

Because my bonuses were computed on my ability to increase total sales volume, I decided to use another system. I instructed my crew never to mention size, just automatically charge for and serve the largest and most expensive item. I even hid all the small and medium cups, because the customers started to point and ask about them. After a few weeks our customers became accustomed to our "one size is all" fast-food restaurant. It was a lucrative system until someone turned us in to company headquarters. It was probably one of my rebellious employees, not a customer. You would have thought it was the end of the world. Every executive in the company had wanted to know what was going on at one of their highest-volume restaurants. I saved my job by destroying every small and medium container we had and told my bosses they were back-ordered. When we reintroduced the small and medium sizes, it confused our customers so much that it took them three times as long to order.

When Renee and I owned our first restaurant, we had to develop many systems just so we would not go crazy. The system we learned from the previous owner was to cook all steaks, chops, hamburgers, and other kinds of meat rare, regardless of how the customers ordered it. The system was based on several assumptions. First, most customers did not know the difference between rare and medium anyway. Second, most rare meats continued to cook to medium from internal heat. Third, most customers who complained did not insist on sending it back to the kitchen. Fourth, we could always cook a rare steak to medium, but we could not fix a steak that was overcooked. Finally, it was much faster to cook everything rare because it took less time and was easier for the cooks to remember. Our customers knew that if they did send a steak or hamburger back to the kitchen, it probably would end up in the fryer until it resembled a burned bacon curl.

We also had a system for cooking eggs. I would crack two cases of eggs every morning at 4:00 A.M. and then whip them up for our omelets. We did not refrigerate the whipped eggs because they cooked faster at room temperature. Of course, when we saw the health inspector drive up, I would toss the eggs into the freezer. I did this not so much to lower the temperature of the eggs but because the inspector seldom looked in that particular freezer. When we first bought our coffee shop, I would whip the eggs with several quarts of half-and-half. But half-and-half begins to sour in the afternoon if left out all morning. So I switched to mixing the eggs with plain water. At the end of the day I would put the remaining egg mixture in the refrigerator. I tried using day-old omelet mix, but it smelled musty and had a slight chartreuse color. Omelets made with the day-old egg mixture tended to be thin, watery, brownish, and wrinkled. We decided to use fresh eggs daily but did not want to throw away our borderline concoction. So we used the day-old eggs in our pancake batter and the leftover pancake batter in the French toast batter.

Cooking old-fashioned oatmeal to order can produce major problems in a busy kitchen. Our customers did not care for the instant powders you can buy in envelopes. I tried cooking real old-fashioned oatmeal to order for a few weeks. When a server placed the order, I would run back in the prep kitchen and grab a small pot. I would fill it with a half cup of salted water and several spoonfuls of oatmeal. Then I would place it on a gas burner while I returned to the front line. Nine times out of ten I would forget the oatmeal and it would boil over, scorch the pot, and plug up the gas orifices underneath. I considered taking oatmeal off the menu.

Then a veteran cook showed me a foolproof oatmeal system. We cooked up a gallon of oatmeal and stored it in quart containers in the refrigerator. When a customer ordered oatmeal we would simply scoop out a serving just like ice cream and heat it in the microwave. Our customers really appreciated the home-cooked quality, and a gallon of oatmeal would last almost two weeks.

Another system we used in the restaurant involved our homemade chili. We would prepare ten gallons at a time and keep it refrigerated. We had a tremendous reputation for our chili, and so did our customers. It actually aged in the refrigerator. We never sealed the lid tightly, because the fermentation gases needed to escape. Ten gallons of chili occasionally lasted several weeks. Our customers liked it better the older and richer it got. One day a group of teenagers wanted two gallons of our chili to go. They insisted on having some of our aged and rich blend. I asked them whom it was for. They said, "Our parents are out of town for the weekend, and we hear that your chili is more fun at a party than alcohol." They mentioned something about a contest and even invited me. Renee would not let me go because she was sure that I would win and humiliate her.

Our chili had a few other peculiarities. You could not cook it in an aluminum pot because the high acidity dissolved the aluminum. One of our aluminum chili pots got so thin that you could almost see through it. You might want to check for any metallic tastes in your restaurant chili from now on. I do not believe the recommended daily allowance is a teaspoonful of aluminum in every bowl. Anyway, you probably already get enough aluminum from your underarm deodorant to be toxic. Our chili also permanently stained clothes and teeth. Some of our customers would eat chili only on their days off, when they would wear old clothes and work outside.

I also want to tell you about a system we used on weekends. We enjoyed a continual stream of customers and were tremendously busy. Weekends were so busy the crew got extremely fatigued and cranky from the seemingly endless and frantic pace. We needed a simple system to close the restaurant when our crew ran out of steam.

We tried closing fifteen minutes early on some weekends and two hours early on others. That did not work because our customers never knew what to expect. We solved the dilemma by hanging a sign on the front door. It read, Open Weekends until the Food Runs Out. After a few weeks that system worked beautifully. Our customers started lining up outside the doors, sometimes an hour before we opened at 6:00 A.M.. It became our most effective and least expensive advertising. The constant line outside our door became a famous attraction, and passersby would stop and line up too. The system allowed us to close almost anytime we wanted with a perfectly legitimate excuse.

Our only rule was that we had to stay open until the homemade hash browns and whipped omelet mixture ran out. At 4:00 A.M. I would prepare gallons of omelet mixture and a hundred pounds of hash browns. If I felt especially tired, I would reduce the quantities and shave off a half hour from our time open.

Our customers always liked to take a chance and try to come in just before we closed. By that time of the day, the cooks were tired and would dump about a pound of potatoes on each egg order so we could close. The omelets also got larger as the day went on. Customers would order one to feed their entire family. The servers knew how to use the system too. They tried to sell every customer an omelet with hash browns once their feet started to hurt.

I would yell across the packed dining room to the head waitress (the same waitress who served cinnamon rolls to Ozzie and me) when we were almost out of omelet mix and hash browns. She would march over to the front doors, bumping and shoving customers, to twist the dead bolt into its locked position. Then she would make a loud announcement to everyone in the dining room: "I don't want any more of those critters coming in the front. The rest of you can go out through the side door."

I was in charge of a hotel and restaurant management program at a community college during the time Renee and I owned our third restaurant. A small café located on campus was used as a student laboratory. Each student would have to manage the restaurant twice each semester. When I took the job, the restaurant had a reputation for slow service and food that tasted "experimental." It also lacked a supply of customers. We needed a model system so the students could be exposed to a successful operation.

Our new system was very simple. We required the students to do the majority of their food preparation the day before. That prevented last-minute mistakes and greatly increased the consistency of the food. On the day of the meal, the entire kitchen crew would do nothing except load and unload microwave ovens. Since it was a student laboratory and we were supposed to be cooking everything from scratch, we used three other small systems to satisfy the administration. First, we disconnected all the microwave buzzers so our kitchen would not sound like an arcade. Second, the students wore all the dirty kitchen uniforms from the day before. Third, we would boil a few pots of water on the stove to make the kitchen steamy. Those additional systems were enough to convince the academicians that we were following established policies and procedures.

Finally, my system for generating more customers was simple. I subtracted one point from the student manager's score for each empty seat in the dining room. We never had a complaint or an empty seat with our new systems management.

7

The First Day

It's Too Late to Back Out Now

I will never forget my first day as a fast-food manager trainee. I walked in the front door and was abruptly told by the assistant manager that employees were not allowed to use the front door. She did not have any trouble recognizing me as one of the new trainees because I was wearing the regulation brown polyester pants, wide brown belt, short-sleeved beige shirt, and ugly brown shoes. I walked to the back of the dining room and knocked on the door, located between the foul-smelling rest rooms. The assistant manager peeked through the security hole and unlocked the door. Quickly closing the door behind me, she said, "Rule number one is always keep this door closed and locked. We've had a few robberies lately." I already wanted to go home and drink wine with Renee next to the fireplace.

The assistant manager took me into a cluttered office that was dominated by a desk covered with coffee-stained reports and cigarette ashes. She gave me a well-used employee's handbook, a plastic name badge, and a paper hat. She said, "You'll be treated just like an hourly employee for the first two weeks. The only difference is that you'll work five ten-hour shifts from 4:00 P.M. to 2:00 A.M. the first week. The second week you'll work five ten-hour shifts with the manager from 6:00 A.M. to 4:00 P.M. Any questions?" I thought about asking her the procedures for resigning.

I detected an overwhelming smell of sweet grease. Not only could I smell it, I could feel it and even see it. Everything in the restaurant was sticky, and all the employees had greasy complexion problems. The grease was coming from two gigantic fryers, which cooked everything from fish fillets to apple pies in the same basket at the same time. I learned to survive in the grease by purchasing an assortment of acne medication and washing my uniforms only with my dog's blankets.

I also learned how to do the fast-food shuffle. The tile floors in the restaurant were always greasy and slick, so everyone learned how to walk without lifting his or her feet. I always thought the shuffle complemented our pointed paper caps and snagged polyester trousers.

After a while I discovered the reason for the belt. Like most other new trainees, I lost about twenty pounds within a month. Many then gained forty pounds when they learned the technique of working less and eating more. The new, ugly brown shoes turned out to be the wrong size, and after I wore them the first ten-hour shift, my big toenails turned purple and fell off.

My first job that evening was cleaning the dining room. I started wiping off tables and stuffing litter into overflowing garbage cans. After I cleaned a particularly disgusting table, a monstrous fellow with long matted hair and multicolored tattoos stepped in front of me. He grunted, "I wasn't finished." I politely replied, "I'm sorry, can I replace something for you?" He said, "Yeah, three double cheeseburgers, two large fries, and a milkshake with double chocolate."

I tried walking calmly to the security door. I told the assistant manager about my problem. She casually stood up from her desk and went to the pay phone in the storeroom. She dialed 911 and told the operator there was a riot in progress in our dining room. Then she walked out into the kitchen and informed the customer, whom we later nicknamed Bubba, that we were not going to meet his demands. A few seconds after Bubba started swinging his fifty-pound arms like a propeller around the dining room, the police and dogs arrived. The dogs barked, skidded around on the greasy floor, and sniffed the tables, customers, and rest rooms.

They hauled off Bubba and pulled one of the dogs out of a garbage can. I finished cleaning the dining room, with help from another customer. He went around to the dirty tables and picked up the discarded sandwich wrappers and other containers, hoping to find something to eat. I noticed he closely watched families with small children, because they often left half-eaten sandwiches and pieces of cookies on and under tables.

I carried the garbage outside to a dumpster surrounded by a creaky fence at the rear of the building. On my way back I heard the dumpster gate opening again. I kept walking and pretended not to hear a thing. I reached the safety of the restaurant and marched directly to the assistant manager. She explained that a gentleman named Al regularly went through the garbage. Al kept the dumpster area neat and clean in exchange for the management's promise not to call the police.

The last thing the assistant manager had me do in the dining room was scoop up the dead flies along the window ledges. I wondered what had killed the flies. Was it the food? Perhaps Bubba was once a gentle and kind person before becoming a fast-food addict. Then I heard a faint blast of compressed air coming from a ceiling corner. It was not long before I could smell the sickly sweet smell of insecticide. The visible droplets floated quietly onto several customers and their sandwiches. I saw a fat fly stall and begin a rapid descent, finally smashing into a speckled window. There it stuck briefly before falling down to the ledge. You might want to observe how restaurant employees clean their dining rooms. Sometimes they start with the window ledges, then the chair seats, and finally your table top, all with the same damp cloth.

I was anxious to finish cleaning the dining room. The crazy customers and poison gas were bad enough, but the thing that annoyed me most was my paper hat. Every time I bent over it would slide off my head. It landed on the floor, on the window ledge, in the garbage can, and even on a customer. I kept screwing it back on my head, even though it was probably dirtier than the floor.

I quickly mopped the dining room floor, which amounted to nothing more than getting it wet. The customers kept walking where I was mopping. They even stepped on the mop head if it got in their way. I found myself hoping a customer would slip and fall.

Months later I learned how to control unruly customers with the mop. I simply used old, sour mop water, and customers would avoid the freshly mopped area like the plague. The assistant manager reminded me to put clean ashtrays on each table. It was important because smokers would grind their butts into the tabletop, chair seat, floor, and walls if there was not an ashtray readily available.

Then the assistant manager told me to stand next to the person at the fryer station so I could learn the position. When we dropped large baskets of frozen fries into the grease, they would explode because of the high water content. The hot grease flew in all directions and usually burned our arms. It took a few days to get used to the fryer burns. I did all right unless I got hot grease directly in my eyes. For some reason it did not hurt as much as it made me sick to my stomach.

I learned to let the frozen fries defrost before putting them into the basket. They would take less time to cook and lose much of their water content. Those first two weeks were a tremendous management training experience, because the employees were teaching me all the shortcuts that I would later have to discourage in my own crew.

I stood at the fryer station for three solid hours the first day, dodging hot grease rockets. My arms began to look as if I had been tortured with lit cigarettes. I had difficulty breathing because my lungs were not used to filtering oxygen through grease. One thing I did appreciate was that my paper hat did not fall off anymore; the fryer grease had plastered the hat to my head. Before moving to the grill station, I went to a mirror to inspect my face. Small yellow balls of grease were clinging to my eyebrows like spider eggs. I also detected the red beginnings of a dozen pimples.

The grill station was simply overwhelming. I could not comprehend the cook's system for keeping track of all the different sandwiches. I practiced wrapping sandwiches as fast as I could for another three hours. It took me about eight seconds to wrap a sandwich. The assistant manager said, "You won't pass manager training until you can wrap one in two seconds."

I maimed and mutilated hundreds of sandwiches. The only ones I was allowed to wrap were those ordered by drive-through customers. The assistant manager knew that we would get too many complaints if my battered and spindled sandwiches went to dining room customers. We certainly did not want another Bubba getting a deluxe cheeseburger that looked like a piece of paper that had been wadded up and tossed into a trash can.

The assistant manager moved me to the drink station for the last three hours of my first shift. It was midnight and we had a shift change, although the new crew was far from fresh. The assistant manager also went home and was replaced by a brittle shift supervisor with a yellow complexion from smoking too many cigarettes. The people in the graveyard crew were not interested in my training. They thought I was a management spy and immediately took me off the drink station and sent me back out into the dining room. I cautiously took one step into the dining room, carrying my cleaning rag, and heard the security door snap shut behind me. There must have been twenty Bubbas sitting in small groups, smoking, and arm wrestling. They all stopped talking and stared directly at me. I thought they had even stopped breathing but reassured myself that had probably happened years ago.

I turned around and tried turning the knob of the security door. Someone came up behind me, paused, and then went into the rest room. I waited for my entire life to start flashing through my mind. I never thought it would end in a fast-food restaurant, with Bubba pulling me into a rest room by my ankle as I kicked and screamed. A merciful employee finally opened the security door and told me to get in quickly. She said, "Never go out there again late at night. Those people will hurt you. That's why we keep all females on this shift. Someone will usually try to help one of us if we get into trouble." I wanted to quit.

I sat in the office and read the ten-page employee handbook over and over for the last hours of my shift. At 2:00 A.M. I carefully walked out the back door, said goodbye to Al over at the dumpster, and quickly crawled into my car. I started the motor and drove the twelve miles home before I stopped, got out, and scraped the mashed double cheeseburger and small order of fries from my windshield.

Renee was waiting up for me with a light supper. I was more interested in a strong drink. She asked, "How was it?" I told her all the gory details of my first day as a manager trainee and spiced it up with a few exaggerations. She suggested that we borrow some money so I could go back to law school, but I was determined to finish my training. I had only twenty-nine more days, half of which were nights, before I would became a certified assistant manager.

I received my assistant manager's credentials and was transferred to one of our units in a small foothills community. I arrived at 6:00 A.M. on the first day. The manager was waiting for me in the dining room. He was a West Point graduate working his way up the corporate ladder. We talked for a few minutes and then a large truck arrived with a week's worth of supplies. Three employees were scheduled to put away the delivery, but they failed to show up. So the manager and I had to do it ourselves. We lifted, shoved, and rolled bundles and cases for three hours. An hour after we started, it began to rain, soaking the delivery before we could get it inside. Can you guess how much a case of wet napkins weighs?

The next four hours consisted of a nonstop lunch rush. The manager asked, "What position do you want to work?" I begged, "Please, not the dining room." To my surprise, the customers turned out to be polite business men and women. On the other hand, I was standing next to some of our employees in the kitchen who could have been off-duty members of an inner-city gang.

My assigned position was backup for the drive-through cashier. She talked to me only once the first day. Just before the lunch rush she threatened, "I don't care if you're management or not. Just make sure I get those drinks fast when I tell ya." She looked like a gang leader and undoubtedly would hunt me down if I ever crossed her.

For the next four hours I was a robot. She would rattle off twenty or more drinks at one time. I would reach down and grab cups from the spring dispensers with both hands. I was in such a hurry that I would squeeze and crush the cups as they came off the sleeve. Then I would take my fist and jam it into the cup to pop it back out. Next I would drag the cups through the ice bin, hoping to fill them with cubes of ice. After the ice, I would thrust them under the drink spigots. Those spigots stayed on continuously for almost four hours, because I had a conveyor belt of cups moving under them.

The only problem I had was the diet cola. It tended to foam and took almost twice as long to fill a cup. The cashier turned around once and told me to hurry up with the diet colas or she would call the manager. I certainly did not want the manager to think I was an idiot, so I filled the diet cola cups with non-foaming regular cola and topped them off with a squirt of diet cola just for taste.

After the lunch rush the manager and I had to operate the restaurant by ourselves, with the help of two part-time employees. We would not get any more help until 5:00 P.M. The restaurant stayed busy all afternoon because it was a Friday and people were getting off work early. We were shorthanded because the manager scheduled his regular afternoon employees for later shifts on Friday and Saturday nights. When one of us had to use the toilet, we temporarily suspended service.

At 5:00 P.M. the evening crew arrived, and I thought we would be able to go home. But the manager forced a tired laugh and informed me that while we were putting away the inventory that morning, we were supposed to be doing the daily paperwork. Also, the time we spent working in the kitchen that afternoon was time normally spent preparing a bank deposit and reconciling cash drawers.

The manager and I played catch-up for the next three hours. Suddenly the shift supervisor came running into the office and told us that an employee had just burned herself on the grill. While the manager filled out the accident report, the shift supervisor and I took over the grill station until we could get someone to answer the phone on a Friday night and come to work.

By 10:00 P.M. the manager and I were about to leave when the graveyard shift supervisor called in sick. One of us would have to stay until 4:00 A.M. The evening shift supervisor quickly volunteered for the job in return for overtime pay and Sunday off. I was the lucky person who took her place on Sunday. The manager and I left quickly, using the back door and not looking back. We were both scheduled for 6:00 A.M. shifts the next day. We took a small luxury and decided to start at 7:00 A.M. instead.

Luckily, I had called Renee, and she was waiting faithfully for me with another light supper. I told her the story of my first day as assistant manager. I was getting used to the business, and she was getting used to my stories. We fell asleep watching television.

Several months later I was promoted to unit manager of a high-volume restaurant. I was excited because managers from that particular restaurant were often promoted to training manager. I was supposed to meet the outgoing manager at the restaurant on a Monday morning. As I drove into the restaurant parking lot, there already was a tangle of cars and people dodging each other. I recognized the outgoing manager sitting in his car, waiting to make a left turn onto the highway. I quickly parked and ran over to his car. He apologized that he would not be able to spend the day with me. There was an emergency at the training restaurant and he was supposed to meet the district manager there at 7:00 A.M. I was also depending on the district manager to help me on my first day. The outgoing manager told me not to worry. He had left a note on my desk explaining everything. I caught myself waving until he was out of sight.

I went into the restaurant and introduced myself to the morning crew. The employees needed help so I worked the counter for a few hours. They complained about their schedules, their pay, and their lives. Out of seven morning employees, three quit my first day. They said it was not anything personal against me. They had just been thinking about it for a long time. I told them it *was* personal and asked if they would consider thinking about it for a while longer. The morning shift supervisor was depressed because she had been the outgoing manager's lover. She also told me she would be leaving in two weeks. I said, "Why don't you stay? Maybe it will all work out." I hoped I wasn't making a personal commitment.

Just before the lunch rush, I received a series of phone calls from suppliers asking for my weekly orders. I had no idea how many eggs to order for the week or how many gallons of mayonnaise to order for the month. I asked the shift supervisor, but she just sobbed, "The manager did everything." I understood. Noticing the first wave of the lunch rush, I called back all the suppliers and told them to deliver the same items and amounts as the week before.

The outgoing manager had left a note on my desk. It said, "Everything is in the file cabinets. Make sure you get the keys and combinations from the shift supervisor. Good luck; you'll need it." The shift supervisor handed me three heavy key rings and explained each one between wrapping sandwiches. I thought I would never remember where they all went, and I was right. She also gave me the combinations to the safes. Tears welled up in her eyes again as she explained how one combination was her birthdate and the other was the outgoing manager's. Those safe combinations had quite a history. I wondered how often the outgoing manager changed them.

Carrying the keys was my next problem. I tried putting them in my front pockets, but three key rings with twenty keys each did not complement my polyester pants. It looked as if my pockets were full of rocks, and I had to tighten up my belt another notch so my pants would not drag on the floor. I bought one of those round, silver key holders with a chain on a spring, the type gas station attendants use. I hooked it on my belt, but the keys were so heavy they stretched the chain out when I walked. I decided to hide the keys in different places in the restaurant. That worked well except when I forgot where I had put them.

I tried the safe combinations, but for some reason they just would not open for me. I asked the shift supervisor to help me. When I watched and she turned the dials, they opened the first time, every time. But when she watched and I turned the dials, nothing happened. Those safes almost had a mind of their own, just like the employees. Speaking of employees, most of my crew also knew the combinations of the safes. Everyone could get the safes open except me.

Somehow I made it through the lunch rush of my first day. I spent the afternoon in the office guarding the money so I would not have to use the safes. A funny thing happened that first afternoon. All the employees started complaining about each other. Every employee, whether he or she worked that day or not, made a special effort to come in and see me. By late afternoon, every employee had maligned every other employee. This political jockeying happens in all organizations and can become very sophisticated. It was enlightening to experience it in its purest form.

My assistant manager arrived at 6:00 P.M. She had been at the restaurant for about four months. She was a delightful person, and I liked her even better when I found out she couldn't open the safes either. We spent several hours talking, and she shared many insights into the crew and outgoing manager. She wasn't looking forward to working with the graveyard shift supervisor. According to her, both the graveyard and day shift supervisors had been the manager's lovers. It seemed that each of the shift supervisors mistakenly thought the other combination was the manager's birthdate.

My first day as unit manager ended at midnight after I met my graveyard shift supervisor. She was whiny and could stick out her lower lip like a two-year-old. On my way home I made a night deposit, and I felt lucky to find the right bank and not get robbed, shot, or mugged. I also thought about how I had not really accomplished anything except listen to other people complain all day. It was one of the most important management lessons in my career.

I was promoted to training manager a year later. Yes, I did finally get my safes open, and I eventually hired a new crew that could not open them.

When I opened the first in a series of new restaurants as a regional vice-president for a full-service chain, I felt very confident and relaxed. Construction was on schedule, and we began hiring our crew. We had some trouble with our gas and water hookups but we finally got hooked up and began testing the kitchen equipment. I wanted to start training the kitchen crew as soon as possible.

One morning things started coming together. Most of the equipment worked fine, and the contractor was laying carpet in the dining room. Our employees had their uniforms, and our food supplies were starting to arrive. It was finally starting to look, smell, and feel like a restaurant.

Late that afternoon I picked up our chairman of the board at the airport. He was interested in our progress and asked when I thought we would be able to open the unit. I told him we could open in five days at the earliest. He said, "I want it opened tonight." I quickly reminded him that construction was not finished and our employees were not yet trained on the equipment. He interrupted, "I don't care about the details, just open the restaurant." He told me to drop him off at his hotel and expect him around nine o'clock at the restaurant for dinner.

I got back to the restaurant just in time to catch the manager and his two assistants going out the back door on their way home. We still did not have a back door, just a frame. I told them the exciting news. We had four hours to get an occupancy permit, prepare the food, and open the restaurant. We decided to give it a try.

The first thing we did was call all our employees. We asked them to come to work immediately. Luckily for us, most of them were available. We put the employees to work cleaning up the sawdust and debris in the dining room. Then we straightened up the kitchen and storeroom as well as we could. In the meantime, the manager cajoled the building inspector into giving us a permit to open.

We devised a plan to survive the first day. It would have been impossible to serve our entire menu. Instead, we instructed our service staff to tell the customers we were serving only sandwiches the first day and their beverages would be complimentary. We turned on the outside lights at 8:45 P.M. and the restaurant instantly filled with customers. We were ready on the sandwich line, and we definitely had enough staff.

At exactly 9:00 P.M. the chairman of the board arrived in a taxi and asked for a window table. His waiter was instructed not to mention the limited menu, and he ordered liver and onions. As soon as we got the order in the kitchen, we dispatched a runner to the supermarket behind the restaurant. Ten minutes later the runner returned and informed us that the market was out of liver. I gave the runner the keys to my car and sent him to another market a few miles away. Almost thirty minutes passed, and the runner still hadn't returned. The chairman finished the salad we had made by chopping up some sandwich lettuce and the soup we heated in the microwave. Finally the runner appeared with a bag, but he said the other market was out of liver too. Instead, he had stopped at a nearby coffee shop and bought an order of liver and onions to go.

The chairman of the board taught me another important lesson. You are really never ready to open a new restaurant. If you cannot just pick a day and open it, someone has to do it for you. He enjoyed his liver and onions and ate it again the next day at the coffee shop where we had gotten it.

So far I have told you about first-day experiences when I worked for someone else. Now I would like to describe the first day of restaurant ownership.

I was supposed to meet the previous owners of our first restaurant at 4:00 A.M. so they could train me and help me through the initial shock. I did not sleep too well the night before and finally got up around two. I drove to the restaurant and parked in a vacant lot so I would not take up any customer parking space. I inserted my key into the front door, but it would not turn, and I could not pull the key back out. I tried jiggling and twisting that stupid key until I felt it bend. I left the key in the door and patiently took all the other keys off the ring. Then I walked around the side of the restaurant and started trying my handful of loose keys, one at a time, in the lock of the kitchen door. I finally managed to unlock the door and went inside.

As I stepped into the kitchen, I felt a blast of heat from the equipment and compressors. I also noticed an overpowering smell of spices and gas. I quickly opened some windows and then turned on some lights. I spent the next fifteen minutes searching under all the griddles, stoves, and ovens for a pilot light that was out. After moving the mobile gas fryer out from the wall, I noticed the smell of gas becoming more intense. The flex hose attached to the fryer was leaking so fast I could even hear the hiss. I gave the shut-off valve a ninety-degree twist.

The previous owners finally appeared and reassured me that flex hoses wear out regularly. I told them about the key stuck in the front door, and they suggested we unlock the door from the inside and just leave the key in it until we called a locksmith. We already had customers coming in the kitchen door, asking for something to eat. I had unknowingly switched on the neon Open sign on the roof. So we turned it off again and told the small group of customers they could either help us open or come back in an hour. Instead, they chose to drink coffee and tell us their life stories while we worked around them.

The previous owners showed me how to fill the dishwasher and told me not to worry about the water leaking from the pump. They said it had been leaking for several months, and a new pump would cost hundreds of dollars. I had brought my toolbox, so I grabbed a socket wrench and tried tightening the pump head. It stopped leaking.

What I found out halfway through the breakfast rush was that the water stopped leaking onto the floor and began leaking into the motor. Instead of learning the dining room systems the first day, Renee hand-washed every dish, cup, knife, fork, and spoon.

About thirty minutes before we opened, one of the previous owners filled a gigantic pot with fifty pounds of potatoes, then lowered it into a deep sink and covered the potatoes with water. Then he lifted the kettle, by himself, out of the sink and hoisted it up onto a stove. It weighed more than a hundred pounds. After the potatoes reached a rolling boil, he turned the stove off and let them cook another twenty minutes with the lid on. Then he showed me how to help him drain the potatoes. He hoisted the pot off the stove and carefully carried it over to the sink. I held a metal lid the size of an automobile tire loosely over the top while he poured off the water. The water was so hot it burned our arms and faces, but neither of us let go. He chuckled, "You'll get used to it. You don't have any choice." What worried me most was that I didn't weigh much more than the pot of potatoes.

We preheated the ovens and quickly separated thirty pounds of bacon strips. The inner layers of bacon were still frozen, and it took longer to pry them apart. We were supposed to open by 6:00 A.M., but we still didn't have the bacon in the oven, the pancake batter mixed, or the eggs cracked. After getting the bacon in the oven, we realized the waitress who was supposed to open the dining room had not shown up. We telephoned and woke her up. She promised to be there in five minutes.

I was worried. We did not get the restaurant open on time, my equipment was falling apart, there was a key stuck in the front door, and my morning waitress was late. I wondered if she ever took more than five minutes to get ready.

I momentarily lifted a fifty-pound bag of pancake batter mix and tried pouring some into a large mixing bowl. I lost my balance and dumped a pile on the floor instead. The previous owner laughed and told me to use the scoop next time. We cracked thirty dozen eggs for the omelets. While I cracked one he cracked four. I would crack a few and then fish out the shells. He showed me how to crack all the eggs first and strain out all the shells later. I was not strong enough to whip the eggs, so he had to do it for me. What was I going to do when he left? Renee would have to do it!

We finally opened and took a few minutes to rest before the rush. I was sitting in the dining room, listening to my breathing return to normal, when I noticed smoke pouring from the kitchen. We had forgotten the bacon, and it was burned beyond recognition. It looked like burned wooden matchsticks floating in a pan of grease. One of our customers shouted, "Burn the bacon again?" The previous owner suggested we use the burned bacon bits for soups and salads. It was very creative of him. We started thawing another thirty-pound box of bacon. Every customer that morning wanted bacon and eggs since we had advertised by smoking up the entire town.

I spent the next eight hours trying to learn how to turn eggs on a grill. I must have ruined over a hundred eggs, and the previous owner did not have any creative suggestions for using them. I mangled pancakes, overcooked breakfast steaks, burned toast, and dropped a plate onto the grill, which shattered it and sent splinters of glass into thirty orders of perfect hash browns. We thought about picking out the glass.

Just before the lunch rush, our prep cook burned the soup, dropped the automatic slicer on the floor, and cut himself while slicing pies. I saw him pop a handful of prescription pain killers into his mouth every few hours. I was surprised when I saw him run the automatic slicer through the dish machine. We sent him home when he started staggering and slurring his words. That was the last time I saw our prep cook. He was arrested that night for breaking into a drugstore.

After the lunch rush, the previous owner told me we should have peeled the potatoes earlier, while they were still warm. I skidded the pot up to the grill area and peeled potatoes between orders for three hours. After two years of practice, I became good enough to peel those potatoes in twenty minutes.

The only other major catastrophe we had the first day was when the milk delivery truck smashed into our main outdoor sign, shattering the neon lights. I called the only sign company in town, and someone there said it would take six weeks to get it repaired. Oh well, the way it was going we did not want to be that busy anyway. The milk deliverer was very apologetic and said his company would take care of the costs. I appreciated his concern but did not care for the marks his combat boots left on my asphalt tile floor. When we closed that evening, I spent an hour on my hands and knees scrubbing off those black marks.

The first day at our first restaurant lasted only sixteen nonstop hours. I ended the day by writing checks to the locksmith, dish machine repairer, and fryer repairer. I bricked the grill and mopped the floors while Renee cleaned the rest rooms and dining room. Finally we spent two hours on our hands and knees picking up a twenty-year accumulation of cigarette butts in our parking lot. We felt good about our business and about ourselves. We had an opportunity most people never get or even want. We were going to do our best, despite the first day.

The first day at our third restaurant was even worse. Renee and I arrived early, along with the employees we inherited from the previous owners. We prepared for a busy day, and I ordered fresh fish, milk-fed veal, and prime rib for the dinner crowd. It was the beginning of a nightmare. We did not have any customers for breakfast. Six customers showed up for lunch, but two of them walked out when they heard the old owner had sold out. The dinner crowd consisted of one couple who had a buy one, get one free coupon from the previous owners. They also insisted on a senior citizen discount. We went home feeling numb and talked about getting out of the restaurant business.

The next morning we did not know what to expect. Surprisingly, we were busy all day and even sold all the fish, veal, and prime rib. We were ecstatic. An employee finally told us why we did not have any customers the previous day: the previous owners were always closed on that day of the week. But it was not long before we were busy every day.

8

Competition

The Art of Counting Cars

When I was eight, I spent the summer selling baskets of apples in front of the restaurant my grandfather had built for my parents. The restaurant had new owners, but they did not seem to mind when I opened for business on their front porch early one June morning.

I gathered some unbruised apples that had fallen from the trees in my grandfather's nearby orchard. I washed and sorted them into small baskets according to their size and variety. Then I carefully loaded the baskets into my wagon and pulled it along the trail toward the restaurant, stopping frequently to kick rocks out of the way and admire the apples.

By 8:00 A.M. my baskets were lined up in front of the restaurant's main door. The owners must have become sick and tired of my going inside every fifteen minutes, asking a waitress for a glass of water. The customers probably were equally disgusted at having to step over me and my apples to get inside.

By noon I had not sold one apple but had taken a bite out of at least a dozen. I had spent the entire morning entertaining myself by taking bites out of several different varieties and watching how fast they turned brown. The sweet apples turned brown faster than the tart apples. I finally traded the cook a basket of tart cooking apples for a hamburger and a Coke.

There was no one in the dining room at lunchtime, and there had been very few customers that morning. I sat at the counter with Bob, the owner, who was smoking cigarettes and gulping coffee thick with sugar and cream. I asked him, "Where are all our customers?" He chuckled and said, "They're all down at the competition." I asked him what he meant by competition. He said, "They get tired of eating here so they try another place." He did not appear worried about getting his customers back. He said, "Competition is good. My customers will be back tomorrow and really appreciate this place after eating down there." He explained how you have to be both good and different to attract customers.

Another reason we did not have any customers that day was that he had just fired a popular waitress and she had gone to work at the competition. The early-morning customers liked her and consequently followed her to the other restaurant. The cars belonging to the early-morning customers who parked in front of the competition lured more morning customers there. The cars from all the morning customers, in turn, lured the lunchtime crowd.

Bob was a seasoned competitor and had already hired another waitress with her own strong following. She was scheduled to start the next morning. He also explained how his former waitress, now at the competition, would benefit him even more in the long run. She had been fired for stealing money and food. I overheard him telling a friend that he had given her a good recommendation when the competitor phoned to ask about her employment record. I would not understand all of it until I got older and had my own employees.

I spent the afternoon shining my apples with a can of lemon furniture polish from the restaurant. I had stopped taking bites because I had a bellyache. I closed my apple stand around 3:00 P.M. and gave the rest of the apples to the cook, who promised me a free piece of pie the next morning. I said good-bye to Bob and told him I would be back in the morning at the same time. He said, "It'll be busy tomorrow, so you'd better bring some extra apples." I did not believe him and was depressed anyway, because it was time for my piano lesson. Why did I have the only grandmother who was a music teacher?

I was late the next morning. It took longer to gather the extra apples, and I rubbed each one up and down on my right trouser leg until it was shiny. I picked only the best apples off the ground that morning and took my time pulling the heavily loaded wagon. Somehow I knew it was going to be a good day.

I lined up my baskets like a fence around the front door of the restaurant and waited. The dining room was already full of customers. I was feeling too excited and serious to take any bites. I skipped lunch and waited some more. By 3:00 P.M. the lunch rush was over, and not one person had bought an apple. Several customers had even kicked my baskets aside with their feet. Even the cook did not want any free apples.

The apple stand across the highway had been busy all day, even though my apples were better and cheaper. I told Bob I would not be back the next morning. I had failed as a businessman, competitor, and human being. My worldly punishment would be a lifetime of piano lessons.

Late the next morning, my grandfather woke me up and told me I had better get my apple stand open. I sleepily explained how my competition had put me out of business, but he insisted I give it one more try. He helped me gather some apples and even picked a few right from the trees. We put them in baskets and together pulled the wagon to the restaurant. The apple stand across the highway was open and busy with customers buying apples and drinking the complimentary apple cider. My competition was both good and different. The sellers were giving the dopey kids free apple cider while their dopey parents bought the apples.

I asked my grandfather if we could give away apple cider too. He said, "That would only help a little. Bob and I have something else in mind." A few minutes later, Bob appeared carrying a large cardboard box. It was full of new-born kittens. He and my grandfather arranged the apple baskets around the box of kittens. By then the mother cat had jumped in too. Then my grandfather nailed a sign onto a nearby telephone post, next to the highway. It read, Free Kittens and Fresh Apples. Within moments the dopey kids at the competition across the highway were pointing in our direction.

I sold out of apples and kittens before lunch. A bleeding heart even took the mother cat. I paid for my own hamburger and my grandfather's coffee that day and explained to the new waitress how you had to be both good and different when it comes to competition.

I had a different perspective on competition when I worked for Joe. As an hourly employee, I was basically confined to either the front or the back of the house. I was isolated, professionally, from the outside world and our competition. But even employees are effective competitors.

I passed through four distinct stages of in-house competition during my thirteen years working for Joe. I do not know if everyone who works for someone else goes through exactly the same stages, but I recognized the same pattern later in many of my own employees.

During the first stage of my employee competitiveness, I tried to work harder and faster than my co-workers. Needless to say, they resented my dedication. In fact, many of them started working harder and faster too. I just hoped Joe noticed that it was I who had started the competition.

I competed with Joe himself in the second stage. I did not have any trouble working faster, but he never seemed to get tired. He enjoyed our personal competition, probably because it seldom happened with other employees. Again, I do not imagine my co-workers were tickled pink about the games I was playing with the boss.

The third stage was a competition with myself. I had challenged and conquered, at least to my satisfaction, the other employees and the boss. Next I wanted to see how far I could stretch my own abilities and limitations. I literally worked circles around the rest of the staff, and they finally slowed down to their usual pace and resumed their indifferent attitude. I was not a direct threat to the employees anymore. They simply thought I was crazy.

Competing with myself eventually became tiring, lonely, and meaningless. I entered stage four. It is the stage of indifference, fierce territoriality, and pettiness. Some employees reach stage four the first day of a new job; others take longer. These stages of employee competitiveness often keep the owner too preoccupied to worry about his outside competition.

When I was a unit manager, I had two sources of competition. One was the legion of corporate ladder climbers who wanted my job and, in turn, my boss's job. The other unit managers in my region were the second source of competition. The performance of each unit manager was compared with every other unit manager's in the same region.

Someone always wanted my job, and I always wanted someone else's. It was stage one of employee competitiveness all over again. But this time it was not healthy competition. My closest corporate allies would stab me in the back without hesitation if it meant a promotion for them. I got used to the frequent coups against myself and my co-workers. But I never understood the long-term grudges and conspiracies, which often lasted for years and usually resulted in minor corporate reshufflings.

As a stage-one hourly employee at Joe's, I was primarily concerned with work and how it would be my ticket to increased challenges and responsibility. But as a stage-one unit manager, I was not concerned with work, challenges, or responsibilities in the same way. I tried to avoid them; I wanted power and authority instead.

Similar to stage two for an hourly employee, I spent most of my time as a unit manager trying to impress my boss and especially my boss's boss. I easily convinced myself that my superior skills were primarily responsible for the success of all my bosses. At one point I became so impressed with myself that I started sending copies of my routine reports to the president and chief executive officer. Again, it was not healthy competition. As a stage two hourly employee, I knew how important the boss was. Joe signed my paycheck, trained me, helped me when I got busy, and became my friend. On the other hand, my corporate boss could not sign my paycheck, did not know enough to train me, was never there when I got busy, and symbolized everything I disliked about the company.

I learned a few important lessons from my early experiences with corporate competition. First, competition was directed inward, as it was when I was an hourly employee going through the four stages. But that inner-directed competitiveness changed from a relatively harmless, productive type to an obviously destructive type. It was destructive to me, my boss, and the entire company. This type of competition is alive and well in our corporations today, and you can buy dozens of how-to books on winning at the expense of others.

Years later I would learn the value of what my grandfather and Bob had taught me about selling apples. It does not make any sense to give your real competitors a paycheck as in intramural corporate competition. It is important to keep your competition directed outward, across the highway. And always maintain competition that is healthy within your company and between companies. This last point is crucial, because we have to work with our co-workers and live with our neighbors.

The second source of competition I had as a unit manager, the other restaurants in my region, was how headquarters judged our performance and corporate value. If one out of twenty regional restaurants was doing extremely well in sales and profits, upper management would interpret that to mean nineteen restaurants were doing extremely poorly. Our competition was considered the *one* successful restaurant, and we were supposed to keep up or surpass it. It did not matter if the one successful restaurant just happened to be next to a family amusement park.

Competing with the other restaurants in my region was like competing with other workers on an assembly line. My crew could work harder and faster, but it was almost impossible to be better or different because the system was directed inward and went only one speed. In other words we were driven by procedures, not by the market.

I managed to experience stage three, although briefly, before entering stage four. As you recall, stage three is competing with yourself. Large corporations have a curious interpretation of this. They usually establish a management-by-objectives (MBO) policy or one of its newer versions. MBO supposedly encourages you to compete with yourself by establishing your own performance goals. This really is not the case, though. Management forces you to participate and to establish goals. Is this competing with yourself? Then management forces you to evaluate your results according to their criteria. Again, is this self-driven competition? Finally, your supervisor undoubtedly is forced by his supervisor to evaluate your own evaluations of your results. This final step squeezes the last drop of self-competition out of the system.

I want to mention quickly stage four as a unit manager. I called this the hourly employee's stage of indifference. Corporate employees also reach this stage quickly and easily but give it a different and more sophisticated name. Corporate stage four employees are called survivors. This incorrectly implies a positive and enviable condition.

Then there is the concept of competition when you own a restaurant. The first thing you will notice about your employees is their inner-directed competitiveness. They will probably feel, just as I did, that they really cannot make a difference when it comes to the competition across the highway. If you let it happen, their work will become mind-numbing routine, and they will care less about your precious market positioning and strategies. How should you manage these competitive tendencies and prevent your employees from becoming indifferent stage-four survivors?

Most employees already will be in one of the four stages when you hire them. It has been my experience that most hourly employees are stage-four veterans with enough ability and energy to make a good initial impression. But it really does not matter what stage your new employees are in when you hire them. You can change them quickly into thinking about the competition across the highway if you do not allow them to think of themselves as independent employees with limited responsibilities.

In all three of our restaurants Renee and I purposely cross-trained our employees so they could help each other when they had a few extra minutes. We constantly made them aware of those extra minutes. We also created a family atmosphere in which everyone was expected to work hard and fast. That family atmosphere was tolerant of occasional emotional outbursts from our employees. Renee and I also had our share of outbursts.

Instead of punishing our employees, we tried helping them with their work and giving them emotional support. Needless to say, this method will not work for everyone and did not always work for us. It did, however, create an outwardly directed staff that was at times more concerned about our competition than Renee or I were. You might say we truly cared for our employees and they knew it. They were our family and our lives. In return, they truly cared for our customers. Our employees were proud that we were one of the busiest restaurants in town. *They* were responsible for being better and different.

Renee and I would sit and talk with our employees early in the morning before we opened. Most of them had driven to work and would tell us how many cars they had seen in the parking lots of the other restaurants. When they drove home in the afternoon and evening, they would count the cars at our competition again. We considered every one of the other restaurants our competition. Even though some of them had different hours of operation, they all took a bite out of the potential three meals a day of every resident and tourist.

Not only did our employees track the number of cars in parking lots, they also tracked the customers themselves. They knew most of the locals in town and also recognized their cars. By tracking their cars from restaurant to restaurant, we could determine what breakfast, lunch, and dinner specials were most popular.

Our employees kept us informed of everything happening at the other restaurants. Restaurant employees have one of the most sophisticated networking systems I have ever known. It is partly because many of them have worked at several restaurants over the years.

They also have their own subculture. Not only did we learn about all the innermost secrets of the other restaurant owners, we also found out more than we ever wanted to know about everyone in town. At first Renee and I felt somewhat guilty listening to all the gossip, but our guilt quickly passed and we looked forward to our early morning employee meetings. The trade-off to that wealth of information was that the other restaurant owners probably were holding their own morning meetings, and we were undoubtedly the subjects of their juicy gossip.

Our first restaurant had an outside window between the kitchen and the dishwasher's station. I could see the parking lots of two competitors through that window and spent many hours counting cars. They always seemed to have more cars, but according to our gossip network, we were busier. One day I counted the cars and then sent an employee over to check their dining rooms for verification. I told him to count only the customers who were eating and not those just drinking coffee. According to our calculations, one-half of the customers in one restaurant were coffee drinkers, while the second restaurant had one-third coffee drinkers. We dispatched the same employee several other times to peek in their windows so we could get an average percentage of coffee drinkers. Once we had an average, we could discount the total number of cars parked outside the restaurant by that factor. It gave us a more accurate and scientific picture of our competition.

We seldom had a significant number of just coffee drinkers, so the method enabled us to compare our eating guests with their eating guests as a function of cars we could count from the window. It was a fast, efficient, and inexpensive way of tracking our competition. One of our servers, who had also worked for the previous owner of our restaurant, used to say to me, "You remind me of Artie. He used to look out that stupid window all day too."

Sometimes our restaurant had an empty parking lot and a full dining room. Sometimes we had a full parking lot and no one in the dining room. That happened when customers from the other two restaurants used our lot. It was incredibly depressing to count more cars parked in front of our competition. We never understood why anyone would patronize them when our food and service were far superior.

Bob was right: people just like to eat at different restaurants once in a while to break the monotony. I would still look out that window a hundred times a day. During our second year, when we started to get really busy, I noticed the owners of the other two restaurants peeking out their windows and counting cars in my parking lot.

The greatest pleasure I received from that window was when my employees started staring out of it and counting cars too. Eventually I forgot about the window. I would just ask any of our staff, and he or she could tell me precisely how we were doing, adjusted by the coffee drinker factor, compared with the competition. They were professional marketing researchers.

Renee and I never ate in any of the restaurants we considered our direct competition. We looked for restaurants that had completely different operating hours and served different kinds of food. Our first restaurant was open for breakfast and lunch, so we ate at a Mexican restaurant and a seafood restaurant that were open only for dinner. We became acquainted with the owners of both restaurants and discovered they ate only in restaurants open for breakfast and lunch. They became our best sources of publicity because they would recommend our restaurant to their customers, and we would do the same for them.

I remember one dark and freezing morning in December when Renee and I arrived at the restaurant at our usual 4:00 A.M.. We started preparing for breakfast while listening to an all-night talk show on the radio. Around half past four, the owners from the seafood restaurant came in the kitchen door carrying an expensive bottle of imported champagne. They had just finished cleaning up their own restaurant after a busy night and wanted to watch someone else work for a change. We drank the champagne together and had a wonderful time talking about the restaurant business. We opened our restaurant a half hour late that morning and felt fine until nine, when the alcohol started catching up with us as we stood over the hot equipment. Several of our breakfast customers came back for lunch just to see how we were holding out.

We avoided our direct competition, including the owners, like the plague after going into one for breakfast on a day off. I could feel the tension mounting as we drove up and I saw all the cars in their parking lot. As we walked in, I noticed they did not have any coffee drinkers and their dining room was full. We ordered and found the food and service depressingly satisfactory. It was a nice restaurant, and it made us miserable. We got the check and realized the food was less expensive than ours. The miserable hostess smiled as we paid and wished us a good day. I turned to look through the dining room as we were leaving and saw three of our most loyal customers having breakfast. Renee and I never again patronized our direct competition.

I would literally bump into my competition at the wholesale cash-and-carry. Restaurant owners are always in a hurry, especially when they are shopping for food. We would load our giant train-station pushcarts with heavy cases and skid around blind corners in the food warehouse. We never spoke to each other. Frequently we smashed into each other at an aisle intersection, causing our top-heavy loads to slide onto the floor or the other person's cart. Sometimes it took half an aisle length just to stop the momentum of a loaded cart. We always watched the checkout lines and waited until they were empty. Competitors do not like to stand in line together either.

I always inspected a competitor's load when we passed in the aisle. I tried to spot items that were inferior quality to those we used. I could pass the information along to my employees and quickly get it into the town gossip network. I also kept track, through the cash-and-carry, of my competitors' average weekly purchases. I could detect any slight increase or decrease in their business. Naturally, they watched my purchases just as closely.

For more than two years, while we owned our first restaurant, I avoided my competitors and they avoided me. If I started to drive into a filling station and saw one of them at the pump, I would pull back out onto the highway and find another station.

Several of us used the same bank. I was a good friend of the bank manager and had established a good line of credit, so I decided not to change banks. Instead, I tracked the times of the day the competition conducted their bank business and simply scheduled my own bank visits at other times. I never enjoyed standing in line behind one of my competitors as the bank teller counted all those beautifully green twenty-dollar bills that should have been mine.

When it comes to competition, there is one thing more exciting than counting cars in parking lots: it's stealing others' best employees. I did not give the idea much thought during the first year of our first restaurant. Renee and I simply did not have the time or energy to do or think of anything except the endless fourteen-hour shifts of cooking, cleaning, and waiting tables. Then we got acquainted with a waitress who worked at the seafood restaurant. We noticed she was efficient, friendly, and full of energy. She was also extremely loyal to the owners, and they trusted her completely, which is almost unheard of in our industry. After several months we asked if she would like to work for us. She thanked us for the offer but said, "No. I like to work evenings, because that's when my husband works." We were disappointed because we had heard from several people that she had a tremendous following.

A few weeks later, she came into our restaurant and asked if the offer was still good. Her husband had been transferred to a day shift and she also wanted to change. That one simple change in our staff probably doubled our business.

I decided if a little was good, more was better. I started looking for the best fry cook. Our new waitress told us that her friend working next door at the competition was the fastest fry cook in town. He had been working there for several months, and the owner had gone to great lengths to recruit him. I asked her to offer him a job at twice the pay. He was interested, but the other owner quickly matched the offer. Our waitress told us he had recently wrecked his car and was having trouble getting to work. I wondered why we were recruiting an expensive fry cook who could not get to work!

One afternoon he came over to our restaurant during his break. I again offered him twice the pay but said I would defer the additional amount toward payments on an old car I had. He could start using the car immediately if he went to work for us. He gave his two-week notice the next day. The new fry cook was just as valuable as our new waitress. He had his own local following. We stopped looking out the window and counting cars after stealing our competitors' best employees. We were just too busy.

As a district manager for a fast-food chain, I saw competition return to inner-directed and regional comparisons. Restaurants were units and were judged against each other. Sometimes we put our best managers in problem units, and sometimes we put them in our best units, depending on the corporate philosophy of the day.

Our unit managers would steal employees from restaurants in their own company. And employees from one of our restaurants would malign the crew of another. You would think our real competition, the other fast-food chains, would be watching and benefiting from our corporate slugging. That was not the case, because the other chains were blindly engaged in their own versions of intramural competition. Ironically, our unit managers were friendlier with the real competition than they were with other managers on their own regional team. In fact, it was common for one of our unit managers to lend food or supplies to a real competitor before lending it to another restaurant in his own company.

My district, in turn, was compared with other districts. The job security of district managers rested on the performance of their districts, just as the job security of our managers rested on the performance of their individual units. My district was compared with every other one in the country, regardless of regional differences or natural disasters.

My district became very profitable after a few months. I started rotating managers around to different restaurants, hoping to develop a spirit of teamwork. Corporate headquarters did not interpret our success as positive. Instead, they just saw the other districts as unsuccessful compared with ours. At the next staff meeting, the other district managers were not overly friendly. A few weeks later, they reassigned district managers and gave my profitable district— with its generous bonus potential—to a senior district manager.

Another thing I remember about the fast-food business was the competition analysis report. Four times a year, each district manager was supposed to visit the real competition. We filled out lengthy questionnaires for a representative sample of our competitors. I would sit in the dining rooms of their restaurants, pretending to eat and read the newspaper, while secretly timing the employees and counting customers. It was silly because one of the employees would tell the manager what I was doing, and he would come out and stare at me as though I were trespassing. I even timed how long the manager stared. It took almost an hour to answer the questionnaire. Then I would casually go up to the counter and order one of every hot item on the menu. The employees would giggle while they filled the huge order, and the manager often seemed to get even more defensive. I repeated this all day and stored the hot food in the trunk of my car.

By late afternoon I would complete my reports and have a sizable mound of food bags in my trunk. My car began to smell like a garbage truck and I could never get rid of the smell between report periods. I would drive back to corporate headquarters with the hot afternoon sun raising the temperature in my trunk to well over one hundred degrees. I could smell the food beginning to cook again. Once I got hungry and stopped by the side of the freeway. I opened the trunk to select a sandwich from the extensive menu, but I changed my mind when I detected the acidic odor of warm mayonnaise.

At corporate headquarters I would unload my bags, which by then would be soaked with grease from the food. Several other district managers on competition analysis duty usually would arrive at the same time, and together we would spread our soggy samples on a large circular table in the executive conference room, which also always smelled like garbage. The executive staff would gather around the table and watch us dissect the food and comment on the products. Sometimes those discovery meetings would last two or three hours, with the food items getting torn apart and put back together again until they all formed a solid mass that resembled a leftover meat loaf.

The result of one particular discovery meeting was to increase the number of pickles from one to two on our deluxe hamburgers, which did nothing except increase our pickle costs. Another meeting produced a taco salad, which resulted in a year of operational headaches. Still another meeting was the beginning of a disastrous breakfast roll-out (the introduction of breakfast menu items) that turned our company upside down and shook out many of our executives along with breakfast.

That was one of the few times anyone in the company ever thought about the local competition. Let's face it, being aware of the local competition just created more problems that we could not handle. Besides, we did not consider other restaurants competitors anyway. The only real competition was their sledgehammer advertising when they saturated the market with television commercials.

Competition took on different meanings as I worked my way up the corporate ladder. As a regional vice-president, my first view of the competition was from an airplane. We would take the company plane and fly over other restaurants in my region. We were looking for the most popular restaurant concepts. We counted cars in restaurant parking lots and analyzed the traffic flow at different times of the day. We also looked for potential sites in front of shopping centers. We did that by flying over the shopping centers early in the morning, before the cars started arriving. The number of oil stains on the pavement was often a good indication of customer activity.

Our company was expanding rapidly and opening another restaurant every ninety days. During that expansion phase, everyone in the company was happy, optimistic, and beyond competition. We thought our concept was so brilliant that no other company would dare challenge our position.

We came to town with bulldozers, marketing specialists, and advance training teams. Once the restaurant was built and before the dust had settled, we opened for business. Then we moved to another location and built another restaurant. We thought our competitors were second-class operations. But as the newness of our restaurants wore off, so did much of their appeal. We found ourselves quickly becoming part of the competitive arena as newer restaurants came to town.

I was introduced to another side of competition during that phase of my career. Large corporate chains tended to compete with the other large chains, medium-sized chains with other medium-sized chains, and so forth. Industry executives also tended to compete with one another. That created some interesting situations. Different companies became bitterly competitive, especially when their chief executives were rivals. It was similar to when I owned the first restaurant. I too was driven by emotions and took everything personally when it came to competition.

Things returned to normal when Renee and I bought our second restaurant. Our employees had an exciting gossip network well established. We avoided our competition by shopping at the cash-and-carry and going to the bank at different times. We even crossed to the other side of the street when walking past the competitive restaurants or their owners. Things did not seem to change when it came to competition. I started counting cars again, until it made me emotionally sick.

It was fun when we would sell a restaurant. Then Renee and I would go into every restaurant that had been our competitor. We would enjoy talking with the owners or manager and realize how much we had missed. It is the strangest feeling walking through the door of your former competition. One day the competitive instinct is there; the next day it is gone.

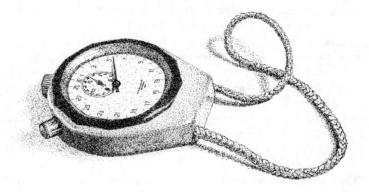

9

Training and Motivating Your Employees

What You Can Learn from the Lion Tamer

I do not think people ever forget their first job. Early one winter evening when I was fourteen, the telephone rang, and I overheard my mother talking to someone about me. She hung up and asked my father, "Joe wants Mike to work tonight and wash dishes. What do you think?" I was mildly surprised when my father replied without hesitating, "I think it's a good idea." Why would he throw me out of the house on a freezing, snowy night? Besides, I had not yet gone through the kitchen eating everything in sight for my after-supper snack. I had never had a regular job, only lots of practice at household chores. I wondered if I would get to keep the money I earned. Maybe my paycheck would go directly to my parents. I worried that it would be a good excuse for my parents to stop my allowance and expect me to help with the mortgage.

My father had been training me with household chores ever since I could remember. He would come home for lunch and write a list of things for me to do when I got home from school. I tried everything to avoid those lists. I even volunteered to stay after school and help clean the chemistry labs. The teacher finally called my father and asked why I did not want to go home. That ended my volunteer work at school.

I tried hiding the paper and pencils my father used for writing the lists. That worked for a week. Then, on Friday afternoon, my father said, "You obviously didn't want any lists this week, so I saved them all for the weekend."

Next I tried being cunning. I would get up early in the morning, before my father, and make sure his coffee cup and newspaper were ready on the kitchen table. I would do a few of the easier chores and also leave a list of those on the table. My intention was to force him to concentrate on my few positive qualities and the fact that I had already been sufficiently disciplined and trained. I wanted Dad to think I did not need any more lists because he had finally motivated me to do the chores on my own.

As usual, I spoiled the charade when I started acting like a machine. My movements became rapid and jerky when I did the unsolicited chores, and I stopped talking to my parents. I imagined I was a trained animal. Dad had pushed me over the edge.

My success rate was holding steady. After a week without lists, Dad said, "This weekend we're going to do all the chores you didn't do last week. And we're going to do them together." That was awful. When I worked with my father, it took at least twice as long. He even expected me to carry on a pleasant conversation with him at the same time! When I asked him why he had not said something sooner, before the chores piled up into a ruined Saturday, he quietly said, "Your mother and I were enjoying the show too much."

Even worse than the lists were the times Dad asked me to help him carry and stack the firewood. We burned about ten cords each winter, and that meant a hundred hours of pure torture. I tried everything imaginable to get out of the work. I would spend an hour lingering on the toilet, feigning a stomachache. When I got back out to the woodpile, Dad would not say a thing. The silent treatment was worse than the work itself.

I was always thinking of a way to make the work easier. Once I tore down a section of fence so I would not have to carry the wood so far. My father did not say anything, and he used the hole in the fence too. When we finished he went inside and told me to mend it. It took longer to repair the fence than it would have taken to carry the wood around it.

So on that cold and snowy night when the telephone rang, Dad knew I was ready to work for someone else. He had trained me by letting me do almost everything the hard way. I will never forget what I learned from his early lessons. First, always let someone with more experience show you how to do something. It will probably be the easiest and fastest way because that person probably learned the hard way too. Second, never underestimate someone who is trying to teach you something; it just prolongs the whole process. Third, carry on a pleasant but not distracting conversation while you work. It makes learning and training more fun. Fourth, always act interested even if you are not. You will get more help from your trainer that way. Those lessons were so simple but amazingly difficult to learn and remember.

My parents drove me to Joe's restaurant that first evening. I remember their telling me to go inside and ask Joe what time I would be getting off. I was nervous, and a half-dozen employees helped me find Joe, who was grating cheese in the storeroom. He said I would be finished by 10:00 P.M. I went back outside and told my parents. Dad said, "Have fun." I actually did have fun that evening—and for most of the next thirteen years I spent working there.

Joe trained me to be the dishwasher. He patiently showed me how to rack and prerinse dishes, operate the machine, and deliver clean dishes to the server